I Am Black Wall Street

I Am Black Wall Street

Doni Glover

Bmorenews.com

DEDICATION

Dedicated to

Amari & Satori

CONTENTS ▌

CONTENTS

FORWARD

Congratulations once again to Doni Glover for putting out valuable information to the black, brown and white communities in this country about the history of the millions of Africans who were brutally kidnapped from their native lands, murderously enslaved and separated in America; robbed of their languages, cultures and families; reduced by overwhelming force to become ignorant, poor and illiterate; made to adopt a version of Christianity that taught passivity, discouraged rebellion and was hostile to their religions; and reclassifed as subhumans who had no rights, opportunities or wealth.

Doni's B'more News is his gift of relevant information to Baltimore's black community, a gift that keeps on giving. Covering a wide range of hard-hitting news about the black community, B'more News has become a reliable Baltimore institution because of Doni's vision, energy, commitment, courage and independence. How does he maintain such a strong voice that gives us the straight scoop in and about a historically racist community like Baltimore?

For his entire conscious life, Doni has been a fearless and unapologetic advocate of black rights, power and history. Like the rest of us in the black community, he has had to educate himself about our suppressed history. His repeated sharing what he continues to learn about our history is his wonderful gift to all of us.

Doni himself will tell you that all of this came from self-employment. He firmly believes that because of the high level of racism in America, black folks can exercise political freedom and the right to speak truth to power most effectively if they are not employees of white-owned businesses.

He knows that we have been the last hired and the first fired. He knows that if racist employers or supervisors learn that you are fighting against racism, they will make you a miserable employee and get rid of you at the first opportunity.

This is one of the reasons he feels that the story of black Wall Street in Tulsa, Oklahoma must be told, retold and retold again. It is the story of magnificent black achievement in the teeth of white racism. But Doni also knows the other lesson: it can all be taken away if if we lose the fight to destroy racism. These are the reasons this book is required reading. Thank you, Doni for this precious gift.

William H. "Billy" Murphy, Jr., Esq.

INTRODUCTION

I have always believed, for some strange reason, that a special kind of blessing awaits the persistent Black entrepreneur in America. I now know why.

We stand on the shoulders of a very long line of titans who literally fought the good fight with their blood, sweat and tears - some of whom even made the supreme sacrifice, so that we may live free and prosper.

This book is not about Tulsa, Oklahoma's Greenwood District, but rather the story behind the story. How did those Black people get to what was then-Indian Territory in the first place? Who and/or what was the impetus?

Before performing the research for this book, I was in absolute awe of the success and accomplishments of the people of the Greenwood District, better known as Black Wall Street. After closer examination, I now possess a better understanding of how it evolved, the continuum of which Greenwood was a part, and the unsung warriors who led the charge to freedom and self-determination there and throughout the Western hemisphere since the 1500s.

All this to say, I have reached the conclusion and can affirm, without a shadow of doubt, that becoming an entrepreneur is literally the most liberating and revolutionary thing a Black person in America can do. In my 55 years of living, I have personally found that there is nothing more gratifying and more empowering than to witness the evolutionary journey of an entrepreneur - that person who has the audacity to risk it all and dare create something viable, marketable and profitable virtually out of nothing. This is particularly meaningful when one considers that the entrepreneurs in question are Black and living in a still racially-hostile 21st century America.

For a person to step outside of their comfort zone, pursue their vision, sacrifice everything, and build a business from scratch is simply a magnificent feat, a journey not meant for the faint at heart. Whether it's a funeral home, like my parents had, or a restaurant, beauty salon, musical recording label, or even a community development corporation, there is something supernaturally beautiful about building one's vision into a profitable enterprise from the ground up and watching it go on to withstand the test of time. Now, for a group of these businesses to successfully band together and grow, in the midst of a mostly Black community in an unwelcoming land like the United States of America in the late 1800s, well – that's called Black Wall Street!

As stated in Proverbs 29:18, "where there is no vision, the people perish." Clearly, the leaders of these people had an extensive imagination for a new and better day in America that included the promise of increased opportunities and room for growth and expansion – far beyond the perils of enslavement. Even the confines of slavery had not diminished their hopes and dreams. Instead, the people of Greenwood rose to the occasion and developed a thriving community.

I have always had this great affinity for business; it comes from my parents. Whether it was answering the family's business phone at age six in my most professional voice, "Good evening, Glover's Funeral Chapel. How may I help you?" or running my own news and marketing firm years later, my entire life has been spent in and around a family business. I can even remember my dad getting copies of *Black Enterprise* magazine in the mail. Sure, I had about 50 other jobs over the years - jobs that taught me what I did not want to do for a living and why; but invariably, there was some enterprise afoot on the home front involving commerce – including my early years as an *Afro American Newspaper* boy.

Through these experiences, I have gained a deeper adoration, appreciation, and respect for Black business owners. As a conscious Black man in America, I am well-acquainted with the historical struggles we have faced and continue to face. From access to credit to redlining to changing laws to a less-than supportive and often betraying federal government, life for the Black man and Black woman in business in America has been and is no crystal staircase.

However, I have also come to know that countless Black people over the years have taken on these oftentimes brutal reigns of entrepreneurship, persevered, and succeeded against all odds despite the boatload of bricks thrown at them. They took those bricks and built communities. I have learned that this entrepreneurial spirit happened in more places than we might realize. Although not well-recorded in American history books, this zeal for self-determination, including the growth and development of Black businesses, is more common than we may think. For some, I personally think it is in our DNA.

Working for oneself offers a certain sense of freedom found nowhere else. I have tried the typical nine to five work schedule. Yet, that entrepreneurial bug was too deep-rooted in my soul. This orientation caused me to turn my focus on this long line of entrepreneurs out of which I come, including those brave hearts who weathered Kansas and Oklahoma just to build a freedom colony. It was mind-blowing research whereby the further I delved into it, the more intriguing the story got, and I realized how there was so much we do not know about our own people – a lot of which would seemingly make most people of any race proud. Those early Black settlers, at least in my mind, epitomized the true power of the human spirit. They left the plantations and sharecropping of the murderous Deep South and headed for a new life west of the Mississippi River.

Even though I have reported on Black business as a journalist for the past 27 years, I have come to realize just how much I didn't know about Black Wall Street and why the story must not be forgotten. My prayer is that our young people might read these pages and come to appreciate and cherish this story, too. Further, it is my hope that the new generation of Black entrepreneurs - like Jessica Howard (Trap Star Vending in Maryland), Kelsey Parker (Think Black App based in Maryland), De'Von Walker (Play Black Wall Street Game ® based in Los Angeles), and Jason Johnson (Black Wall Street Charm City based in Maryland) – will come to know that they stand on the shoulders of giants, and that if those ancestors could prosper in times as vicious as the 1800s – then surely we can succeed today!

Uncovering Hidden Black History

When I first established the online news flagship, *www.bmore-news.com*, back in 2002, I knew that an online publication had to also have a physical presence in the community – just like a newspaper. Websites were relatively new at the time, and thus, for people to even know we existed, I surmised 'off the break' that *Bmorenews.com* had to do more than just post news articles. I was certain that this business had to literally touch people.

I had to go above and beyond the basic expectations of a news outlet to effectively engage people through this novel 21st century technology in order to make it a highly interactive experience for visitors. The goal was to keep people coming back to *Bmorenews.com*. I have always believed the notion that while business is a good thing, repeat business is everything! At the time, I decided that one of the best ways to effectively engage people was to create a platform to bring about invaluable business encounters.

We began hosting monthly business networking meetings at either Black-owned or Black-friendly (ones that hired Blacks) establishments along the Baltimore-Washington corridor. We called it the Harambee Dinner Club. 'Harambee' is Swahili for "all pull together". Our theme was: "Come together, break bread, and network." I would be negligent if I failed to thank Charlie Dugger, a retired Baltimore City educator, who introduced me to the term more than 40 years ago when he introduced me to the airwaves at Morgan State University's *WEAA* 88.9 FM. The vision was to put our advertisers in direct contact with potential clients at regularly hosted business networking events. It made sense that if we were able to connect our advertisers with new potential business prospects effectively and expeditiously, it would be a win-win situation for all involved. And it was.

By 2011 or thereabout, I had just come into officially learning about Tulsa's Black Wall Street. Sure, I had heard of the GAP Band's song, "You Dropped the Bomb on Me" (The Gap Band, 1982). However, like countless others, I did not put two and two together. I did not realize that singer Charlie Wilson was referring to an actual event. I thought it was simply a song about a love relationship. I had no idea that bombs were literally dropped on this most magnanimously-built Black community in the Greenwood District of Tulsa featuring some 36-square blocks with approximately 600 Black-owned business between May 31st and June 1st, 1921.

Social media played a huge role in my learning. I saw a graphic on Facebook featuring facts about Black Wall Street, including "600 hundred businesses". While I had a respectable (or so I thought) understanding of the early history of Black entrepreneurs, I came to realize that what I knew was only the tip of the iceberg.

Initially, I remember asking myself, just what would induce a group of people to bomb and burn down the entire Greenwood District in Tulsa that resulted in over 300 hundred Blacks killed, 10,000 more displaced, and hundreds of Black-owned businesses totally destroyed?

The Black Wall Street story consumed me. Always in the re-invent mode, and ever willing to pay homage to this crown jewel of US Black history, I decided to start giving away Black business awards at our monthly dinner meetings in remembrance of these ancestors. After all, Black business is one of *Bmorenews.com's* five tenets: Black business, education, ex-offender services, affordable housing, and universal access to health care.

We hosted our first Black business awards ceremony in Washington, DC at Busboys & Poets in the fall of 2011. Our partners on the venture were Sisters 4 Sisters Network, Inc. under the leadership of Peggy Morris. Another early awards ceremony was held at the United Nations in

New York, thanks to Bob Ingram, Marsha Jews, Odessa Hopkins and Peggy. Initially we called it The Black Capitol Awards. My mindset at the time was that of creating a national Black business award to celebrate entrepreneurship. Remember, Black Wall Street was still new to me, yet engrained in the back of my mind.

Origin of the Joe Manns Black Wall Street Awards

As I was being influenced by what little I initially learned about Tulsa's Greenwood District, the original award's name soon morphed into the Joe Manns Black Wall Street Awards. Joe Manns is the owner of the award and trophy shop located in Gwynn Oak, Maryland. He and his son, Josh, make the now coveted awards.

Without the generosity, cooperation and support of Joe Manns, who knows what would have happened. Joe and Josh are the kindest people in the world and exemplify in my mind the kind of businesspeople we all should be. Joe is the absolute first to give back to the community. I should also mention that it was Leamon Best who first directed me to Joe. Leamon is a blind man who has hosted several talent shows in Baltimore for years. Having attended one of Leamon's ceremonies where I was an honoree, I noticed that he had a table with about 200 trophies for awardees; 200 large trophies. I had never seen such a spectacle. Nor had I ever imagined just how powerful this blind man was. Instead of feeling sorry for himself, he went out there and helped empower hundreds, if not thousands. Honestly, I thought to myself if Leamon could make such an impact, then so could I.

With the year 2021 signifying a century since Tulsa's Greenwood section was hatefully and brutally destroyed by a mob of jealous whites, it became critically important to me to re-visit the story of this community because not enough people know about the sacrifices of the Black people in Greenwood, especially in an otherwise racist America.

Even more importantly, too few understand that although Tulsa's Greenwood section was the economic development jewel of Black America, it was just the tip of the spear. Truth be told, there was some type of "Black Wall Street" or Black business district most everywhere

Black people lived. Because of segregation and the tactics of the Jim Crow era, Blacks were forced to do business with each other because Blacks, at the time, could not shop in white stores.

For the uninitiated, Tulsa's Greenwood community was considered, pound for pound, one of, if not the wealthiest Black community in America between 1906 and 1921. Furthermore, while Greenwood is commonly referred to as 'Black Wall Street', there are also two other official Black Wall Streets in America. One is in Richmond, Virginia's Jackson Ward, made famous by the likes of Maggie Lena Walker. Walker is the first woman of any color to charter a bank in America. The other is in Durham, North Carolina and the noted anchor institution behind it was North Carolina Mutual Life Insurance Company, one of the oldest Black insurance companies in the nation.

Greenwood District, unfortunately, was not the only thriving Black community tragically attacked. While some may think the events of January 6, 2021 at the Capitol Building in Washington, D.C. signified the first time people attempted to overthrow the American government, the truth is that the first and only successful coup d'etat in American history was the Wilmington Massacre of 1898 in North Carolina (Evans, 2021). It devastated a thriving Black community. Black businesses were destroyed. Black elected officials were literally chased out of town. And as many as 300 Blacks were killed. This was not just two people fighting on the corner (Lafrance, 2017). This tragedy was a planned conspiracy by violent white supremacists determined to destroy Black progress where, in the end, more than 2,000 Blacks left Wilmington (DeSantis, 2006).

I believe that the more this broader Black Wall Street history is shared, the better the chance of Black entrepreneurs across America gaining a heightened sense of their people's history of self-empowerment and self-determination. To learn that one's ancestors were able to effectively navigate the horrific social issues and brutality of the day, like slavery, massacres and lynch mobs, and yet still emerge to build viable Black business communities beyond compare is mind-blowing, and is, I think, quite enough to motivate a Black entrepreneur today.

Greenwood also helps dispel the stereotype of Blacks being lazy, worthless, lacking vision, unskilled, and unsuccessful. Nothing could be further from the truth. Additionally, the more I examined Greenwood and the key players, like founding father O. W. Gurley, the more I realized that Greenwood was not just the most recognized Black business community in America. It was part of a much broader continuum. It represented a centuries-long journey of a beautiful people's struggle for the right to be, to compete, and to succeed no matter what.

It was Rev. Michael Carter of Black Wall Street USA headquartered in Oakland, California who first taught me about Gurley. In researching Tulsa's Greenwood District, I came across Carter's international social media network on Facebook that he and his team built. Carter also made it clear to me that God was at the center of Tulsa's Black Wall Street's success then and must remain so now if we are to succeed in our quest to help strengthen America's Black businesses. He said that the people of Greenwood could not have achieved such success without keeping God first in their lives. Frankly, I believe the same thing holds true today. If we keep God first, we can do anything but fail.

I soon learned that there were "Black Wall Streets" or Black communities all over the United States that many of us have never heard of, particularly in the eastern half of the country. This, according to my research, would essentially reflect a map of the Chittlin' Circuit, where Black entertainers and musicians performed typically before Black audiences during the era of Jim Crow. What was really fascinating for me was how far west this network of Black communities or towns extended. Even more, learning about Greenwood compelled me to find out more about the Black Wall Street history and environment in my own hometown, Baltimore, beginning with my parents' family business.

As this broader vision of a map of economically strong Black communities across the country is being formed in my head, I started to see similarities: the Black corner store, the Black beauty salon and barbershop, the Black church, the Black bank, the Black newspaper, the Black lawyer, Black organizations/societies/brotherhoods, and, of course, the Black doctor. In short, the more I learned about Tulsa's Black Wall Street, the more inspired I was to share the story with others. The Joe Manns Black Wall Street Awards became a natural fit as a platform by which to do this.

The awards celebrate Black entrepreneurs and professionals as well as the people who support them regardless of race. We've honored every race, including at least one Native American, entrepreneur and speaker Milton Hunt.

To date, we have honored over 1,700 individuals in several US cities, including: New York, Baltimore, Washington D.C., Richmond (VA), Atlanta, New Orleans, Chicago, Detroit, Miami and Tulsa. We've visited New York City, Washington, D.C. and Atlanta several times over the past decade. Many thanks to our powerful partners across the country. In Miami, there is Joey Noble, in Houston, there is Kofi Taharka, and in New Orleans, there is Corey "Bing" Mathis, son of Frazier Mathis (Globalvessels.org founder, and the same man who took me to Ethiopia and Tanzania).

In Atlanta, many thanks to Robert Scott, Janice Paschal, Carlos Forde, Morocco Coleman, and Bou Khan. We also have a wonderful crew In DC and Gorgeous Prince George's County, including Prince George's County State's Attorney Aisha Braveboy, former Mayor Carol Johnson, Beverly Smith-Brown, Micheline Bowman, Jennifer Hamilton, Tawanna Terrell, Will Hopson, Mayor Eugene Grant, Dr. Wilbert Wilson, Mark Spencer, Esq., Stan and Terri Long, Alfred Isaacs (the king of MBE policy) and WOLB's Coach Butch McAdams.

In Baltimore, many thanks to my entire city – and the county, too. There are some who give unconditional love without question, like Angela Beard Hardy, Janet Arce, and Minister Lutisha Williams. Special thanks to Rhonda Watties, Glenda Curtis, Kenny Brown (mentor extraordinaire), Sanjay Thomas, Keith Martin, Ty Lawson, Darius George Hall, Andra Cain, Thomas Hardnett, Mike Haynie, Jimmy Britton, Xavier of Xavier Furs, Tony Randall, Minister Corey Barnes, Julius Henson, John Bugg, Officer Evan Anderson, Officer Chuck Lee, Larry

"Pop Pop" Gaines, Marshall Cullens, Kevin and Kathleen Setzer, Attorney Billy Murphy, Attorney Robert Dashiell, Attorney Ivan Bates, Attorney Kisha Brown, Attorney J. Wyndal Gordon, Attorney Neil Dubo, and Judge Alexander Wright. Mike Posko at Chesapeake Habitat for Humanity, one of the greatest human beings I have ever met, has also been a great help. Joey Brown at Baltimore's historic Joseph H. Brown Funeral Home and Derrick Jones at Derrick Jones Funeral Home: *Thank you for always having my back!* Renny Bass and KC, the Godfather, are great supporters and have never left me hanging. Robert Harrington of R.E. Harrington is not only a supporter, but he has a giving heart like I do; he cares about these young people. Bishop Barry of Bishop Barry Pest Control cannot be forgotten. Andy Bertamini is a blessing; he always reminds me of the infinite possibilities in life. Jake Oliver, what a journalistic legend – right along with Charles Robinson; these two keep me honest. This serial entrepreneur is doing certified business up and down the East Coast. There is no way I can forget my oldest homeboy alive, Stephen Shakoor Davis. Shot-out in heaven to my other oldest homeboy and friend, Anthony Marcellus "Marty" Williams.

In Michigan, Tia Chanel (my hero) in Flint and Pam Perry of Pam Perry PR in Detroit have been simply a joy. In L.A., special thanks to Troy Rawlings. Also on the West Coast, I cannot forget my former college roommate at Morehouse and my biggest critic, Friends School graduate Leonidas Hyman, Jr.

We have been so successful at spreading the word about Black Wall Street since 2011 because of these people – and many like them. Because of their generosity and support, over 1,700 awards are out there in the universe. Even more, the message about Tulsa's Black Wall Street is being discussed now more than ever. And I love it. Finally, we are getting it. Finally, we are embracing ourselves like never before. Teamwork makes the dream work!

Correcting Revisionist History

The goal here is basic, yet robust. It is to share with readers what I have learned from my research and maybe even inspire some budding entrepreneurs to push forward on their dream, no matter how bold it is. The hope is to bring some context to the history of the Black business mindset, something that has always existed but is rarely discussed.

This book is neither intended to be any sort of seminal study on Black business nor any type of groundbreaking body of work. It is simply intended to spread light on what I find to be empowering history with the hope of inspiring new, young, Black entrepreneurs who might be struggling to find their way – something to which I can personally relate very well. If anything, this is a re-cap of some information that we should have been taught early in school.

Learning about Tulsa helped me realize just how much I did not know about Black History, particularly in the realm of business, and why I needed to use my craft (media) to help disseminate this information to the masses.

As a life-long student of media, I've found that Hollywood often paints Black people in a derogatory manner that stereotypically places us on the periphery of any scene. Yet, history reveals time and time again that Black people have always been leaders and have always aimed for excellence - even in a place as brutal and unforgiving as America.

And so, while Hollywood has yet to properly undo these misconceptions fed to us for the past century, that inevitable task is left for Black writers, authors, and filmmakers. If the Black Wall Street story is to gain wings, then we must be the ones who tell it from our own perspective. Otherwise, the history books will never properly reflect the entire picture, including the courage and the dignity of our journey. All that future generations might think is that our only legacy is slavery.

Au contraire, dear reader! There is so much more to the story!

You see, I believe if our ancestors could run businesses and run them well amidst the racial hatred back in that cold and vicious time period, then certainly we can do it even better today. I also think that all Black people in America today, quite frankly, must have a heightened business acumen in all aspects of life because our very survival depends on it.

I think we, as a people, must move beyond being solely great consumers and focus more on becoming great producers once again. America is about capitalism, and it is high time we come to learn the game and learn it well. Otherwise, we will keep getting "played" and manipulated. As they say, 'you're either at the table or on the menu.' I say, it is time to focus more on being the boss and owning a string of restaurants!

Let modern day American history books tell the story, a picture has been traditionally painted over time that negatively depicts Blacks. D. W. Griffith's "The Birth of a Nation" is the quintessential example because it set the racist precedent for mainstream media (Griffith, 1915). As a result of this mindset, Blacks in America have been historically characterized as docile, subservient, clownish and anything else except heroes in America.

These portrayals are so far from the truth because the Black man has the oldest history on earth. Hence, he is anything but a follower. Further, he has always led, explored, sailed, created, and invented. Yet, that's America for you. It has always been about the business of diminishing the impact of Black people far and wide. To White America, we are depicted as savages – much like any other non-whites. The interesting thing is that if anyone has been the savage over the past 500 years, it is White America.

America's history books have done a number on both Blacks and whites alike. For instance, Americans tend to think that all Blacks were slaves and that all whites were free in the country's formative years when chattel slavery was legal in America. This assumption is not true. There were white slaves and white indentured servants who are hardly ever mentioned. Moreover, there were also Black people who were never enslaved at all. Again, this is rarely mentioned – unless you know someone like Dr. Helena Hicks in Baltimore. A leader of one of the first anti-segregation sit-ins in the country in the 1950s, Dr. Hicks is an extremely proud Black historian who can trace her own family's history back 300 years without one mention of any of her ancestors being slaves (Hicks, 2014).

The overarching purpose of this book is to open people's eyes to truths that have been hidden in plain sight. This is 2021, one hundred years since the Tulsa Massacre. The game is over. People are awakening to the lies told to us for the past five centuries. As people realize these truths, I believe that the lies will lose their power and fade to darkness, and the natural balance will be restored.

While mainstream media often paints Blacks as violent criminals and murderers today, real Black history teaches us that Blacks have always had superior mental faculties, including a penchant for business, engineering and technology. I am reminded of the richest king who ever lived, the African emperor Mansa Musa of Mali (Mohamud, 2019). I am also reminded of the Dogon people of Mali who were studying the stars thousands of years before a telescope was even invented (Sullivan, 1985). America has blinded so many of us for so long, we do not realize the greatness out of which we have descended. My goal is to help us see the bountiful beauty, living legacy and glorious luster of our ancestors. If we knew more, I believe we would be headed to a more self-sufficient and self-determined future.

I'm no shrink, but common sense tells me that if you consistently tell a person or a people that they have no culture, no history, no value, that they are nothing, no more than a thug in a rap video, and then reinforce it with terror – such as that behavior exhibited by the Ku Klux Klan and other violent, domestic hate groups in their lynching of Blacks across the South or the constant police killings of unarmed Black people today, then it is conceivable that eventually that person or people might develop a warped sense of self. Some may even believe that they are insignificant and consequently carry on with a diminished sense of self-worth. I see it all the time.

America has been horrendously cruel to Black people. It is highly conceivable that we collectively have a horrifically damaged self-esteem because we have endured an endless onslaught of trauma, including so many negative images in the media bombarding us since childhood. Many Black folks, quite honestly, are simply worn out. Noted psychiatrist and author Dr. Frances Cress Welsing's *Isis Papers* and renowned author Dr. Joy DeGruy's *Post Traumatic Slave Disorder* both addressed this history of trauma inflicted by whites and the subsequent ramifications generations later. Clearly, the effects have wreaked havoc on the Black social structure, beginning with the nuclear family.

Dr. Welsing's dear friend and Baltimore-based colleague, Dr. Patricia Newton (who passed away during the editing of this book), spoke about reversing this downward spiral all the time during our many one-on-one conversations. A world-renown psychiatrist, Dr. Newton will always be dear to me. After all, she is the one who prophesied nearly 20 years ago that I would travel to Africa. And she was right.

The point I am making is simple. Black people throughout the Americas have been extremely disaffected by an insidious institutional racism. Five hundred years later, both Black America and White America are still trying to pick up the pieces and achieve some level of clarity with knowledge of who we are. Unfortunately, America is addicted to racism like a drug addict. You see, we have yet to address the 800-pound gorilla in the room – America's original sin: slavery. Even if all of the Black people in America get therapy, it won't matter if White America never admits its problem. Racism has to be called out by name. And reparations must be made.

I happen to unapologetically think that Black people are so much more than what is depicted in the mass media and what too many of us unfortunately have come to believe about ourselves. Part of our collective healing is recognizing the lies, misinformation, and propaganda that have been heaped upon us for centuries.

Now, on the other hand - if you constantly give a person knowledge of their people's powerful past and the contributions of their ancestors; if you help them to see that despite the whip, the noose, and the rapes – our ancestors were able to build successful institutions and maintain a sense of community anyway, I believe our backbones will get a bit straighter, our minds will become clearer, and our souls will become purer and free to pursue our heart's desires. This is much the same vision espoused and demonstrated by noted Pan-Africanist Marcus Mosiah Garvey, considered a "notorious negro agitator" by J. Edgar Hoover of the Bureau of Investigation, precursor to the Federal Bureau of Investigation (History.com Editors, 2009). Garvey showed that Blacks could accomplish anything, including The Black Starline shipping company and the *Negro World* newspaper. His Universal Negro Improvement Association was the largest organization of Black people in the world with 1,000 chapters in 40 countries.

Both Americas have been living under lies for far too long, and that while Black America clearly has work to do on itself, so too does White America. Too many whites lack knowledge and understanding of their fellow Black Americans' contributions to the building of America – including the fact that Black soldiers have fought in every major battle this country has waged, including the Revolutionary War where the First Rhode Island Regiment is believed to have helped tip the scales of victory. I believe if whites knew more of the truth, that light would chase away a lot of the generational darkness and racial hatred rooted in ignorance too many have harbored within their families for generations.

Sit back and prepare to be enlightened by this necessary and timely read. Prayerfully, the reader will discover some hidden gems of Black history and maybe even become inspired to tap into that entrepreneurial spirit within. Better yet, this book might encourage others to become better human beings.

Let me just add, as an entrepreneur myself, it is my personal belief that every American ought to have a business. A business is an excellent tax vehicle from which to improve one's financial health. I would also add that one might even consider eventually launching a non-profit organization, too. I believe it was Joe Haskins, CEO of the Harbor Bank of Maryland (a 51% Black bank in Maryland), who first introduced me to the model of having a non-profit along with a business some years ago. He noted that, if worked properly, the two can co-exist and blossom wonderfully down the road.

For me, business is the embodiment of America and entrepreneurship is a mindset that we, as a people, must all come to better understand and embrace. We must come to highly appreciate our $1.9 trillion in annual disposable income and begin the shift from being super-users to super-manufacturers and super-producers. We must also help spark that same business-minded/entrepreneurial spirit in our children and grandchildren. We can, and we must plant those seeds early in their lives simply by leading by example. Each one, teach one. And each one pass it on. That's what Black Wall Street means to me: that although I did not live in Tulsa, I AM BLACK WALL STREET, TOO!

A Black Wall Street
State-of-Mind

In order for Greenwood's Black Wall Street to become the most talked about Black business community in the nation in the early 1900s, Black people had to be, generally speaking, on the same page. Clearly, they collectively had a deep sense of self-determination. They knew they needed each other. They knew their individual roles, both adults and children, as well as their collective responsibility for Black Wall Street's success.

Such self-determination is still revered today because it is not often that we see such a monumental success as that which was found in Greenwood, one clearly rooted in cooperative economics.

Can you imagine "all Black everything"? Well, that was the mindset of the people in Tulsa's Greenwood District, the jewel of Black America. It is the attitude, belief and conviction that despite all of these ills presented to Black people by America in the name of institutional racism, we too, can build our own communities and also compete in the marketplace – and not just stateside, but globally, as well as our white counterparts. And if we can't, we'll die trying!

Whether you are a barber, a graphic designer, a maintenance man, a secretary, a web developer or a would-be author or playwright, this story is for you! If that entrepreneurial bug has been nagging at you, then possibly, these next pages might just get you jump-started on a project that you have pondered for way too long. Procrastination accomplishes no legacy worth remembering. There comes a point in all our lives when we must go for it – just like those early Blacks in Oklahoma and Kansas. As is told, 'nothing great comes from comfort zones.'

Our ancestors across the Western Hemisphere demonstrated for us how to be pro-active with a strategic plan and to execute at the right time without hesitation. After all - no guts, no glory!

Further, let me just say that I have been among the strongest proponents of the political process in my community since the mid-90s. I have toiled for over a quarter century covering elections and politics throughout the State of Maryland. My experience also includes media coverage of the White House on a few dozen occasions. The task was to break down politics for the everyday person and keep them informed. With the White House only 45 miles away, it is one of *Bmorenews'* way of staying relevant. With that said, let it be known that in light of these efforts to help educate and inspire Blacks in the realm of politics, I personally put a hell of a lot more faith in the power of Black business development. I guess I'm growing impatient with politics.

Simply put, we are all alone out here. No one is coming to save us. "We are all we got!" Applying the lessons of Tulsa's Black Wall Street to our current dilemma, I think, is the most viable solution to improve our plight as a people. I believe that the more we control our resources and our spending, the better we can prepare for our future as a people. If the Trump era has taught us anything, it should be that we had better get on the ball with our finances and we had better do it now. Even more, we must get back to being producers, manufacturers and landowners as opposed to being super-users (top consumers) and renters. Lastly, we cannot be afraid to look at doing business in other countries, including in South America and Africa.

After years of observation, I can earnestly say that we have not learned the game of politics well enough to play at the big table. We are playing checkers while our white counterparts are playing chess, if not poker. We are still new to the machinations and nuances of the political game; or one could even say that we have been effectively marginalized. At the end of the day, my point is that we had better realize quickly that we must do for ourselves economically because no one is going to do for us what we can and should do for ourselves.

A lot of people in Baltimore did not like President Trump talking bad about our city and blaming our plight on Democratic politicians. While he is somewhat correct on that one, Trump lacked the credibility to talk bad about our city. He is the last person on earth to talk about anyone, especially considering the childish, bigoted behavior he demonstrated as Commander-in-Chief during his reign of racial terror. And let us not even get into the slumlord charges against the Trump empire.

Nonetheless, if politics is not bringing back money to the Black community, then it is a waste of time. Other than a 'feel good' moment, what else is politics bringing us? What is the return on our political investment? What are our demands? What did we negotiate? And, by the way, just what is our agenda?

Blacks saved the Biden campaign which was on life support prior to the South Carolina primary and turned around and saved the day, thanks to the likes of Stacy Abrams in Georgia. There should be immediate rewards for these deeds.

I think Black people need to take a page out of that same book as many foreigners who come here and focus more on economics. Having a boatload of Black elected officials in Maryland, for example, means absolutely nothing if it does not translate into money, jobs, business development and overall expansion for the Black community. To their defense, the community has to do a better job supporting Black politicians, too. Relationships are a two-way street!

Over the past 50 years in Baltimore, I have seen the Black community at a standstill while the neighboring white communities breezed right past us in terms of project development. The political will in Baltimore, in my best estimation, has never been wholeheartedly committed to re-developing Baltimore's Black communities. I should add that Baltimore's first elected Black mayor, Kurt L. Schmoke, did lead redevelopment efforts in East and West Baltimore in the 90s by way of the $100 million federally-funded Empowerment Zone, but we have seen very little since then.

As a marketing specialist for Empower Baltimore Management Corporation from 1999-2002, I saw first-hand what an infusion of $100 million in resources can do for otherwise forgotten parts of the inner-city. Much of the focus was on job creation, increasing home ownership, and business development. This impacted thousands individually and God knows how many more when one considers the families positively affected and empowered. It was truly a great period of renewed vigor in Black Baltimore. Never before had funds and resources come to the Black community, and unfortunately, none since. Many of us wonder if that level of electricity in the Black community will ever happen again.

At the present rate, gentrification is seemingly too well-set in motion to be reversed. The concern is that soon, Blacks will not be able to afford to live in places like Sandtown, the historically Black community in which I currently reside in West Baltimore, nor in East Baltimore (another traditionally Black community). While Baltimore may be the last East Coast city to gentrify, the groundwork has already been laid and seemingly, it is just a matter of time before Blacks are priced-out.

Nonetheless, with $1.9 trillion in annual disposable income nationally, I think Black America has all it needs to succeed. Remember, we are victors and not victims. Regardless of the threats and challenges, nothing can stop a determined people – especially one that fears none but God. We just have to get more folks on the same page of supporting Black businesses and Black institutions like we used to do. Otherwise, we are no more than beggars sitting on bags of gold.

Quite honestly, I think COVID-19, President Donald Trump's racially divisive politics, and the horrific murders of Breonna Tayor, Ahmaud Arbery, George Floyd and others in the spring and summer of 2020 – along with the subsequent "Black Lives Matter" protests around the country and globe have helped re-catalyze and better galvanize an even stronger voice for Black America. "Black Lives Matter" is being discussed around the globe. So too is "Black Businesses Matter". I see the sleeping giant awakening after a long, 500-year slumber and its return is poised to make history with our young people leading the way.

Today, I see a resounding interest nationally focused on protecting Black progress. I see an effort on behalf of Black people by Black people – and others – where part of that mission is a focus on Black economics. This I love! A prime example is the song "Entrepreneur" by Pharrell and featuring Jay Z. This song and the respective video capture the sentiment of what we truly need to be doing. And that means stacking our dollars and turning them over in the kinds of businesses we need and deserve in our communities.

As pointed out in the video, the late rapper Nipsey Hussle truly encapsulated and exemplified the type of community-oriented economic mindset necessary to reverse the negative plight of the Black America. I think Nipsey clearly displayed that we can buy back our communities, build our own businesses, and employ our own people. That's a Black Wall Street state-of-mind in my book, all day long and twice on Sunday!

In an August 2020 Rolling Stone article, "Pharrell, Jay-Z Challenge Systemic Racism on New Song 'Entrepreneur'", Elias Leight writes:

> Jay-Z and Pharrell Williams reunite on "Entrepreneur," which the pair released Thursday at midnight. The song is accompanied by a new music video that spotlights black men and women, including Tyler, the Creator and Issa Rae, who have started their own businesses. "Entrepreneur" is "all about how tough it is to be an entrepreneur in our country to begin with," Pharrell told *Time*. "Especially as someone of color, there [are] a lot of systemic disadvantages and purposeful blockages. How can you get a fire started, or even

the hope of an ember to start a fire, when you're starting at disadvantages with regards to health care, education, and representation?" Pharrell directly addresses racial inequality in his whispered verses: "The system imprison young black boys/Distract with white noise." Jay-Z discusses the lack of equal representation for minorities in media — "Lies told to you through YouTubes and Hulus/Shows with no hues that look like you do" — and advocates for supporting black-owned businesses: "Black Twitter, what's that? When Jack gets paid, do you?/For every one Gucci, support two FUBU's.

Whether it means boycotting a racist business or supporting a newly-opened Black business, Floyd's death – in many ways, has helped spark and rejuvenate a new day and a new movement re-focused on the empowerment of the Black community. It's kind of like a reincarnation of the 60s.

The point that I really want to bring home is that we can use what we already have, including 21st century technology, to better solve our own dilemma as a people. That's one thing I got from the blockbuster "Black Panther" movie. We all saw a future with us in it ... finally! That movie helped counter over a century of negative, stereotypical mainstream media images and sounds that have been insidiously thrust upon us since "The Birth of a Nation" to sway both white and Black opinion.

If anything, COVID-19 has made it perfectly clear that we'd better look out for ourselves because there are still those bitter spirits who relentlessly want to vote us 'off the island' our ancestors built. America still has wicked people like former Minneapolis Police Officer Derek Chauvin who would kneel for 9 minutes and 29 seconds on a handcuffed Black man's neck until he died face down in a gutter while calling for his mother in his dying breaths.

For me, Black Wall Street is simple. It is a mindset, a way of life, and a movement. And it involves every member of the Black community as well as those from the outside who similarly support it. Black Wall Street, to me, is about self-determination. It is about taking trade and commerce by the horns and making it work for the Black community in America and beyond. It is time that we take all of the knowledge from all of the degrees we have posted on our walls and use them to effectively build up the Black community.

Black Wall Street means Black people supporting Black businesses – anywhere and everywhere ... by any means necessary and with zero excuses. And with today's technology, entrepreneurship is becoming an increasingly viable option. Even more, this 21st century technology makes it even easier for Blacks to support Black businesses. A person can simply "cash app" their purchase in a matter of seconds. At the same time, we have to be mindful of just how powerful we are and careful not to use that power to empower others before we empower ourselves. Master P, for instance, cautioned Black people when "Clubhouse" was valued at $1 billion. "I keep telling people, we go on Clubhouse, we making another one of them a billionaire," P said in a video posted on Instagram. "We just did it! Just for Clubhouse. We need to create stuff like that to where we control the narrative and we're able to put the money back in our community and our culture (Saint-Vil, 2021)."

Black Wall Street is the thinking that I will support Black businesses no matter what. It also means that if I cannot help a Black business, then I certainly won't go out of my way to hurt one. If I cannot help a Black business succeed, for example, then the last thing in the world I need to be doing is blasting them on Facebook. Like our elders have taught us, politely pull them to the side and express one's concerns. If I can't help them, I won't hurt them. Prayerfully, they will figure it out.

Yep! Black Wall Street is a state-of-mind, an attitude that promotes a way of living that is historically sound, culturally in-sync with the ancestors, and, generally speaking, just plain ol' common sense. Every other ethnic group in America understands group economics and supporting their own. The goal here is to inspire Black people to get back to doing the same thing and also to help breed and nurture a whole new generation of young, socially-conscious and historically-astute Black entrepreneurs.

Let me just add that although I have very little faith in politics, this is not to suggest at all that we not be involved politically. To the contrary, it is imperative that every Black person understand the interrelationship of politics (the process of determining who gets what, when and where) and economics (the allocation of scarce resources). It's called political economy. We deal with it all day everyday whether we realize it or not. The late Maryland Congressman Parren J. Mitchell was a champion nationally as he spearheaded the federal government 8(a) program in 1978. It called attention to the massive disparity in terms of Black businesses' ability to access federal contracts. This changed the game for thousands of Black businesses and helped to create new Black millionaires. Consequently, Maryland became the first state in the nation to create a minority business enterprise business development program.

Truth be told, every Black person ought to know every elected official representing their community. That includes the City or County Councilperson (local), the Mayor or County Executive (local), the Governor and Lieutenant Governor, the state Senator and state Delegates (state), the US President and Vice-President, the Congressperson (federal) and the two US Senators for that state. It is incumbent that we have their cell phone numbers and email addresses, as well as those of their staff. We must also attend and support their functions, including fundraisers. Further, we must understand how legislation can change policies that directly affect us. And we also have to have an agenda. As they say, 'the squeaky wheel gets the oil.' 'A closed mouth don't get fed.' And, 'you have not because you ask not.' This is what we have not mastered just yet: setting an agenda for our elected officials, monitoring them, and holding them accountable. And this includes writing op-eds to local and national news outlets when necessary. Whatever it takes, we must build relationships with the agents of change. And if they do not know what to do, we may even have to actually teach them. I've done it a few times.

Put simply, we get what we negotiate. Quite often in politics, Black people are predictably too slow on the draw. While we are still in the planning stages, the other team has already executed their plan of attack and is going back for seconds. By the time we get to the table, the turkey has already been carved up and there is nothing left but scraps. We saw it happen in the first round of Stimulus monies for businesses. The big dogs ate well while the little ones scrounged around for scraps, in many instances.

This is where the expertise of a former State Senator, Joan Carter Conway, in Baltimore is missed now more than ever in Maryland. She was the quintessential Black elected official who still wields a mighty sword in Annapolis, the state capital. She understands how to get things done. This unapologetically Black woman served our community extremely well and led us to many victories we might not otherwise have accomplished. This is a part of the Black Wall Street state-of-mind, also! More than anything, I most appreciate Conway because she is a business owner. For me, and this is just my own idiosyncrasy, I happen to believe that an elected official who has run a business for 30 years is better-qualified to think broader and act bolder than an official who has no entrepreneurial background at all. I also believe that they are more likely to understand my needs as a business owner and they're better able to advocate on my behalf. Again, if the Black businesses are thriving, getting business opportunities, growing their capacities and credit-worthiness, the better it is for the community. People get hired. Families get stronger. Cities begin to heal from within.

Be that as it may, the bottom line is that the political deck is heavily stacked against Black people. Therefore, we must begin to: (1) Better comprehend and understand the political process and the political machinations that actually get and keep a candidate elected; and (2) We have to better appreciate and understand the need to support our Black-owned media outlets so that the people's voice is always heard and never muffled. Certain mainstream outlets tend to paint an ugly image of my community while giving other communities a complete pass. These same outlets present a sterile, corporate perspective of our beloved Black community as opposed to one birthed out of a genuine love and concern for the people. These are just some thoughts on the need to be more politically astute. More than anything, we cannot forget to pass these practices and observations on to the next generation.

I just believe that if you have Black elected officials worth their salt, then that means that Black progress is being pushed forward. Period. If progress is not happening, then the words of the late Mayor for Life of DC, Marion Barry, come to mind: "Vote the bums out!"

Marion Barry, former Mayor Maynard Jackson in Atlanta, former US Commerce Secretary Ron Brown – these giants ensured that Black businesses prospered locally, nationally, and internationally. They set the gold standard for where we should be today. Bottomline: If politics isn't bringing back the bacon, then somebody does not understand power. Further, it takes all of us to be involved: parents, teachers, students, community leaders, journalists, lawyers, doctors, nurses, and the trashmen. Everybody! Teamwork makes the dream work!

3

Passing the Torch

There is a young man in Los Angeles that I recently met. His name is De'von Walker and he and his wife created the Play Black Wall Street Game ®. I pray that he knows just how proud of them I am for not only creating this product, but for having the foresight and wisdom to even think of such a marvelous idea. I pray he understands that this Black Wall Street Movement is not about any one individual and how critical it is for each one to teach one.

There is another Black man, Rashid Aziz. His building is not far from my home. It's called Citywide Youth Development's E.M.A.G.E. Center and is in the 2100 block of West North Avenue – roughly three blocks from Penn-North. Penn-North, of course, was the epicenter of international media attention in the spring of 2015 when Freddie Gray died in Baltimore. This $3 million center, the by-product of political support from both sides of the aisle, includes a manufacturing plant with a couple hundred sewing machines. It also has silk screen pressing, retail space, a restaurant and office spaces. The center is run by young people. For me, it is amazingly delightful to the eye. This center is the home of Made in Bmore Clothing and Frozen Desert Sorbet; I wish we had these kinds of businesses all over the country.

And that is the ultimate hit: To pass forward this knowledge of Black Wall Street and Black History in general to our young people so that they can take that history and run with it. We really must do a better job as a community building bridges with our youth – self included. And that's why the E.M.A.G.E. Center is so important to me and should be replicated across America.

I just want the next generation of Black businessmen and business-women to be indoctrinated into the history of the Black Wall Streets across America at a very young age as was I. In fact, Black Wall Street history ought to be mandatory in American public schools. I want America's youth, in essence, to grow up as I did with a Black Wall Street state-of-mind where the doctor, the corner store owner and the insurance man were all Black. And I want them to understand how there was a time when everybody knew their role. The Black politician had a role. The Black business owner had a role, too. And so did the preacher. I think our ancestors had a mastery of playing team ball, a mentality that we need to re-embrace today. After all, we can accomplish more by working together.

I also need our youth to know about Black icons like San Francisco's William Leidesdorff, officially the first Black millionaire who became a powerful force in California, and an astoundingly brilliant Annie Turnbo Malone, entrepreneur, the Matriarch of the Black hair care industry, millionaire, educator and philanthropist extraordinaire who mentored Sarah Breedlove, better known as Madam C. J. Walker.

I want our beautifully gifted Black youth to also know about the boldness of Jesse Binga to open the first Black bank in the North (Chicago) in 1921. I want them to know that despite the ugliness this world might throw at them based on their skin color, that there are numerous ancestors who not only faced worse odds, but also had the audacity to be successful. These legendary souls are our heroes and are to be revered by all. In fact, Hollywood should have movies about them, their courage and determination, and their exceptional contributions.

So, welcome to my report on America's Black Wall Streets, and what I've learned over the past decade about a topic of discussion that should be more commonplace – at least in my mind – particularly in the Black community.

Hell, even Trump was talking about Black Wall Street.

4

Critical Thinking 101: Countering the Mainstream Storyline

There is an indomitable spirit in the Black entrepreneur that is rooted in the souls of the ancestors. No matter what, come hell or high water, if there is anyone who will survive the storm, it is the Black entrepreneur. To say the least, I am eternally proud to be one.

America's history books have miserably failed us all because they've told us what they wanted us to know, not the complete story. Consequently, too many Americans lack the facts and consequently have little appreciation for the contributions and achievements of Black people in America. In the process, many of us have forgotten how strong and innately united we are. It is my hope that as we learn more about our history, the more likely are our chances of success in an otherwise hostile environment. Frankly, we have not seen hostile; not like our ancestors.

Where unity was once the norm in the days of my youth in the late 60s thru the early 80s, many of us have since become increasingly American-ized, more integrated and more comfortable. Too many of us have mentally surrendered and have all but forgotten the struggle and how we used to be.

We have become more individualistic. We seem to have more of a 'me, myself and I' mentality today where it's all about the 'Benjamins'. We also seem to increasingly lack interest in coming together as a people. Hell, we barely even have family dinners like we once did. This frame of thinking is constantly reinforced via the music we hear and the television and films we watch, especially the ever-depressing local news.

While Dr. Martin Luther King, Jr. and Rosa Parks are staples in our typical history texts here in the USA, there are countless other stories about our accomplishments, our victories, our heroes, and our heroines in which we know very little. If we did know more about these phenomenal and awe-inspiring ancestors, I wholeheartedly believe our world perspective would be improved and our trajectory as a people would be augmented towards higher ground.

This is especially meaningful when it comes to our youth. As the adage goes, "If we knew better, we'd do better!" That is probably why I've committed my life to Black media – to help tell a more accurate depiction of "Black Excellence" amidst historically white hatred and institutional racism. Our young people need a deeper sense of who we are and from whence we have come.

I have personally concluded after nearly three decades as a journalist that many of our greatest contributions to humanity have been hidden, stolen, or destroyed. It's as if some people are too afraid to allow these truths to be widely known, for to do so might cause some enlightenment in an otherwise dark, taxing and institutionally bigoted landscape. And surely, the racist white powers that be could never have that! Oh, no! Thus, I can unequivocally say to every one of my readers: Do your own research! Think for yourself! Trust your gut. Use your brain to think things through critically for yourself. Don't just believe any crock of crap thrown at you! Do not believe what anyone, including me, tells you about anything. Go and investigate for yourself and draw your own conclusions. You will be glad that you did. Critical thinking is essential to our survival.

For instance, in my research, too often I've found docile and stereotypical images of our ancestors that are derogatory, dehumanizing, and demeaning. They portray our otherwise proud and rich lineage instead as inferior, ignorant, cowardly, underdeveloped, irrelevant, and lacking intellect – let alone spirituality. I submit that this ignorant notion is so far from the truth, that in fact, African History is World History, and that without the African, that story of mankind cannot possibly be told with any credibility.

Yet, we still have a lot of us who willfully subscribe to these negative notions of ourselves. "White is right. Black is back. Tan is grand." "Black people will never get it together." "Get a Jewish lawyer." "Africa is a shit hole." "This is a white man's world." "Black businesses ain't shit!" These things are not true and hold no power over us when we already know the truth for ourselves without any outside interruption.

5

Role of Social Media in My Awakening

Around 2009 or so, I was encouraged by a dear colleague, Alexis Coates (AlexisCoates.com), to join Facebook. (He has since pushed me onto other social media, too.) I am so glad I took his advice because it opened a whole new world filled with the unlimited exchange of information with people from around the globe. I found that my soul so desperately desired such a quenching of information. It wasn't long after that I came across a post about Tulsa's "Black Wall Street", all that had been accomplished by its citizens, and how all of it was destroyed starting on May 31st through June 1st, 1921 in approximately 15 hours by a mob of angry and jealous whites.

This was all new to me. I had never heard the term before but I sure did like the sound of it. It sounded royal, majestic, and definitive. And the more I researched, the more I came to revere what Black people – African Americans, Moors, Hebrew Israelites or whatever the appropriate/politically-correct term for melanated peoples is – built in the 1800s and early 1900s. While I knew a few tidbits, the story of the Black people in Tulsa's Greenwood section would usher me into a much deeper grasp of Black history.

At some point, it dawned on me that the GAP Band had been telling Black America about Tulsa's Greenwood section since 1982. For one, who knew that GAP is really an acronym for Greenwood, Archer and Pine – historic streets in Greenwood which were the roots of America's most significant black business district? I sure didn't!

For the longest, I thought the song was detailing a love affair, that is, until I realized that bombs were literally dropped on Greenwood in a deliberate attempt to destroy the most amazing business accomplishment by my people in this land we call the United States.

Mind you, it took me a while to wrap my brain around the Tulsa massacre. So, having never heard of the story, I began doing research, including reaching out to colleagues around the country to see what they knew about Tulsa. To my surprise, although many people knew nothing about Black Wall Street in Greenwood, I also found people who were well aware of Tulsa as well as the broader history of Blacks in Oklahoma.

Lastly, as a Black media professional, it is imperative to me that the lopsided tales that we have been told for generations are once and for all corrected and forever more widely disseminated. This just doesn't include Black history; it entails the history of mankind.

From the San Bushmen of Namibia, who have the oldest DNA on earth (Connor, 2011), to Luzia in Brazil, a Black woman whose 12,000-year-old bones were discovered in a cave and are the oldest bones found in Latin America, the truth is that the African is indigenous to every continent on earth (BBC, 2018). To omit the Black man and Black woman's role in history is a huge flaw of Western history texts. Thus, America produces a lot of college graduates with a distorted indoctrination who tend to believe that Christopher Columbus "discovered" America in 1492.

Fast forward to my days at Coppin State University in the mid-90s: The very first assignment my media class at Coppin State was given was to watch "The Birth of a Nation" by D. W. Griffith. Professor Ronn Nichols insisted that we understand that as future Black media professionals, ours was the arduously daunting task of perpetually countering this racist, non-Afrocentric dogma by telling a more precise account of events than our mainstream counterparts.

In essence, he assured us that we would have an uphill battle in telling the clearer truth in an America and a world that has been anything but kind to Black people by ways of Western media. In so many ways, we have been seemingly written out of history while others have been inserted. Christopher Columbus' 1492 journey is the quintessential example: How can you possibly "discover" what was already founded thousands of years prior?

However, Nichols had a way of compelling us to follow that truth, no matter how difficult, wherever it should lead us. And for that lesson, we are forever grateful. We now know that the history of the Black man and the Black woman are essential to any legitimate discussion pertaining to human history. Without them, there is no story.

6

Early African Presence in the Americas

Until the philosophy Which hold one race superior and another
Inferior, Is finally And permanently Discredited And abandoned
Everywhere is war. Me say war.
- War, Bob Marley and the Wailers (Marley, 1976)

As for Tulsa's Greenwood District, I wanted to know how it came to be. There are plenty of books already on the magnificence of Greenwood, such as those by Hannibal Johnson. I wanted to take a different approach by looking into the story behind the story – you know, the stuff that's left out of history. I wanted to know, first and foremost, the origin of those first Blacks in Oklahoma. I also wanted to know what brought them to Oklahoma. One of the first things that blew my mind was how Tulsa's Greenwood District was one of 50 to 70 Black towns in Oklahoma. And this is exactly where the research took on a life all its own.

It forced me to revisit what I thought I understood about American history. Today, gladly, I have a better grasp of how the story unfolded and a better sense of what was going on at the time. To say the least, there is so much to understand about those early days in America. There is so much we just don't know.

In other words, it was not as 'black and white' as we tend to think. It wasn't, for example, just white colonists coming here from Britain and slaves brought here from Africa. People were coming here from various nations, as had been the case before the arrival of the first Europeans. Yet, America never acknowledges any of this. Truth be told, many of us have no clue about what was happening here in North America in the year 1300 A.D. – primarily because there are no widely-known written records.

Upon embarking on this mission to understand the history behind Tulsa's Black Wall Street, the goal was to uncover the little-known information about the unsung heroes and the untold stories which laid the groundwork for this jewel of Black America to ever be.

I soon came to realize that the exceptionally successful Greenwood District did not just happen out of thin air. In fact, it is a part of a long continuum of freedom fighting efforts by Blacks on this side of the world going back centuries to secure our own – too often in the face of war, slavery, and racial hatred.

Further, it became quite evident from my research that often these strides for freedom and self-determination involved armed conflict. Sadly, these stories are not taught in our schools. Instead, a more sterile version of history is set before the masses.

To effectively grasp the actual history of the Americas since the arrival of the first Europeans, one must understand, from the top, that Black people have been in the Americas for thousands of years, going back to Luzia, the name given to the female remains found in a cave in Pedro Leopoldo, Brazil in 1974. This is a stark contrast from the typical American storyline of the first Blacks coming to the Western hemisphere in the hull of a slave ship.

When non-Blacks tell the story of the Black man in the Western hemisphere, too much is often omitted, like the history of these Black Indigenous Americans, i.e. Black Indians. And so, this is one thing about this broader story of Tulsa that has captivated my attention from the very start - the relevance of Black Indians in Indian Territory which, of course, later becomes Oklahoma. This is of particular interest to me because my paternal grandmother was Blackfoot Indian and my maternal grandfather was Puerto Rican, making me part Blackfoot and part Taino. Further, since I was a lad, I have always had a deep appreciation for Indigenous peoples – even without realizing my own ancestry at the time. I just always felt a connection to the history of the so-called Indians and loved to see them kick butt in Western movies growing up.

In an article, "True First Americans: Califians (Khalifians) and the Poisonous Thanksgiving", writer Jae Jones writes:

> History about the first true Americans has been manipulated and influenced by Europeans for hundreds of years. Today, these lies in history continue to be told in history books across the country. Information about African history has always been limited or omitted to benefit Europeans. The truth is European people arrived in America, manipulated Africans and Native people; stole from them; used them as slaves; and killed them. African American history has always been told through the eyes and words of the Europeans. According to best-selling author James Loewen in his book "Lies My Teacher Told Me," nothing but lies have been taught in school about the history and civilization of America. If it is not corrected now, generations to come will be subjected to the same lies and lack of knowledge about the country's history.

> To believe that civilization began when Europeans arrived and brought it to America is absurd; it just didn't happen that way. (Jones, 2018)

In a recent interview with Dr. Esther Pearson of Massachusetts, I asked her what tribes had Black Indians. She said that all tribes had them (Pearson, 2021). Although she is a trained mathematician, scientist, and engineer, she is also the author of *Black and Red Roots: Discovering Your Native American Ancestry*. The book was written out of her desire to learn more about her own background. What manifested was a guide to help other African Americans to find out their own ancestry.

Many African Americans have family stories that were passed down from one generation to the next which include references to Native American ancestry. These stories were passed down from the elders in a matter-of-fact manner. The conversations went something like this, "You know your great grandmother was an Indian", or "Remember grandpa. He was an Indian". These facts were accepted without dispute or fanfare as simply another part of the rich African heritage and then African American life. But, as time went on, curiosity about the Indian family roots generally took hold and evidence of the claims of Native American ancestry was sought. This book will guide you through your journey to finding or discovering your Native American ancestry (Pearson, 2019).

Hence, there are two important facts to consider from the very beginning. First, there were Black people already here in the Americas on their own land when the European first arrived. Thus, as these European invaders entered North America, what may have started as peaceful eventually turned violent. The truth is there were then two groups of Blacks as the slave trade evolved; the Indigenous and those brought here from Africa to become slaves. This is particularly meaningful as some tribes are later officially recognized by the US government and granted compensation for their lost land while others are not recognized at all and some were even relegated as slaves.

And, of course, slaves were typically not entitled to any rights or compensation for their land. What's fascinating to me is the development of the Dawes Commission where whites actually determined who was Indian and who was not based on skin tone and hair texture (Osburn, 2010). Imagine that! Imagine someone determining that you are not of a particular people although the evidence says otherwise. That takes a lot of gall. Yet, that's exactly what happened.

Secondly, freedom ain't free. Blacks have had to fight for survival in the Western Hemisphere, I imagine, from the very first interaction with the European. Clearly, no one in their right mind wants to be a slave nor give up their land. No sensible person wants to work for free, have their children work for free, have their wives breed children to human traffickers, or be beaten, raped and maimed. No one wants to be degraded or treated like they are animals.

Quite naturally, Blacks resisted slavery and colonization as any sane people would. Blacks resisted the same way American settlers resisted the taxation of Britain. And, although not typically discussed in American history books, it is for certain that wherever there was slavery, best believe there was a Black warrior king or warrior queen planning either an insurrection or an escape. And they did! Some even formed Maroon societies/colonies. Originally an 18th–century term meaning "lost in the wilds", these Maroon or freedom colonies existed throughout the Western Hemisphere and provided a safe haven for Blacks who escaped slavery.

These bold ancestors – known and unknown - are forever our heroes for all eternity all because they had the audacity to fight back. And that is exactly the level of energy necessary to grow a successful business in America – especially if you are of the darker hue. It is indeed a fight, and one that arises on multiple levels: mentally, physically, spiritually, economically, and politically.

Additionally, the more we know about our lineage, the less we fall trap to someone else's definition of us. The more knowledge of self we have, the less likely we are to become lost in someone else's opinion of us because we already know our history.

7

Early Freedom Colonies in The Western Hemisphere

While the Spanish, Portugese, French and English have all extensively documented their histories of exploits in the Americas, the full story of the Black man in the Americas is less known. American students are officially taught that the first African slaves in what is now the United States were kidnapped and brought to the British colony of Jamestown, VA by Portugese slavers on August 20, 1619 for sale.

This misinformation could lead one to think that these Blacks were the first Africans in the so-called "New World". Further, there is the lingering assumption that surely, the first Blacks in the Western hemisphere certainly had to be slaves. Additionally, there is virtually no mention of slavery in the rest of the Western hemisphere as if slavery only happened in the United States. These points could leave an American student in the dark with a parochial perspective on the broader reality of the Trans-Atlantic Slave Trade and how these events and developments really unfolded (Sertima, 1991).

Pedro (or Pietro) Alonzo Nino, for example, was the Black Spanish explorer who piloted the Santa Maria during Christopher Columbus' first visit to the Americas beginning in 1492. Yet, there is little if any mention of his name (Cassidy, 1959).

Juan Garrido, an African conquistador from West Africa, is actually the first recorded Black man to step foot on North American soil in La Florida (Florida) with a Spanish expedition headed by Juan Ponce de Leon in 1513. Previously, he was in Santo Domingo (Hispaniola), Puerto Rico and Cuba (Gerhard, 1978).

Another noteworthy Black man was Estevanico, also known as Esteban or Stephen the Moor or Mustafa Azemmouri. Estevanico was the Moroccan explorer who, around 1527, became the first Black man to explore North America in modern times. He went from Florida all around the Gulf, including Arizona and New Mexico, on the Spanish Narvaez expedition. He is described as "the first great African man in America" (Herrick, 2018).

It should be noted that slavery in South America began with the Spanish and the Portugese over a century before slavery blossomed here in the US.

What I have always found interesting is how just prior to Spain and Portugal's exploratory years across the Atlantic where they would eventually take slavery to a whole other level, parts of the Iberian Peninsula had been dominated by the Moors, Black North African Berbers, for nearly eight hundred years. While Black Moors were considered royalty across Europe for centuries, made significant contributions to European culture and even built some of Europe's first universities in that period, a seismic societal shift occurred whereby the Black man soon became culturally dethroned and utterly regarded as the number one slave in the world. Further, religion played a key part in all of this as there was much hostility between Muslims and Christians at the time.

Nonetheless, despite what is generally known about Blacks in the early Americas, there is one key part of the story that is rarely told. And that is the history of freedom colonies. If one allows American History books to fill in the blanks, one will get the distinct impression that after Europeans brought Blacks to the Western Hemisphere for the purpose of slavery, one day, miraculously – the European slavers suddenly realized their wrongs, grew a conscience, and nobly decided to do the right thing and abolish slavery.

The traditional storyline could leave one with the distinct impression that somehow Blacks almost embraced slavery until the bitter end

– as if our beautiful Black ancestors took to slavery like it was second nature. The truth of the matter, though, is that there have always been those Blacks who resisted the vicious horrors of servitude with every fiber in their being. Some enslaved Blacks elected to literally jump ship, preferring suicide over a life of torture. Some mothers killed their own babies to spare them a lifetime of misery. But there were also those unsung heroes and heroines of the struggle for freedom who had the audacity to fight back – whether that fight should take place on land or water.

What's more, it was not uncommon that among the enslaved were African kings, queens, princes and princesses. Sarah Bonetta Forbes, "Queen Victoria's African Princess", is among the most noted (Kiste, 2018). Caught in the trappings of the slave trade, she was an Egbado princess of the Yoruba people of West Africa who eventually became goddaughter to Queen Victoria. The point is that just because the ancestors were enslaved did not mean they lost their royalty or their ability to lead.

With this stated, the fight for freedom was perpetual. It never ended. Wherever there was slavery, there were also slave rebellions. And when those escaped Black people reached safety, they established Maroon societies or freedom colonies. The Portugese called them quilombos, meaning "war camps".

The Truth Revealed: What do you know about the history of the Black people in the Gullah Islands along the coast of South Carolina and Georgia? Their history goes back beyond 1619 to June 1526 when the actual first Africans were kidnapped and brought to South Carolina by a Spanish slaver. Two months later, the slaver was dead and the Africans had escaped. They are considered the progenitors of the Gullah peoples, who still live there today (Brockell, 2019).

Did you know that escaped Blacks were living free in Gracia Real de Santa Teresa de Mose, Florida (St. Augustine) in the 1600s (Landers, 1990)? Did you know that free Blacks were living on Burlington Island, New Jersey as early as 1659 in a place dubbed the "Cradle of Emancipation" (Roncase, 2016)? So much of our proud history has been hidden from us.

Yet, slowly but surely, the truth is being revealed and what was buried is now rising to the top for all to see. Despite the lackadaisical and buffoonish images of Blacks since the early days of American media, the truth is that the very presence of a conscientious Black man and woman has often spawned fear and intimidation in racists fearing backlash for their dastardly deeds. And so, there are several strong and resistant Blacks who have never been celebrated in America nor well-recorded in her history books.

Alex Haley's *Roots* provided many people across the nation with theirs first glimpse into what American slavery looked like. Most people who remember the television series recall the story of Kunta Kinte, Chicken George and Kizzy. However, there is so much more to the Black journey in the Western hemisphere.

So, while Western media often gives us a sterilized version painting Blacks as docile and subservient, the truth is that a dynamic, ride-or-die heroism runs deep in our bloodlines. Despite all of the negative images of Blacks in Hollywood films over the years, please know that there have always lived some Black freedom fighters who would not stop fighting until they were either free or dead. And this was the case from the very beginning.

KING BAYANO (PANAMA) Some of the earliest Africans forcibly brought to the Americas in modern times landed in Panama with Vasco Núñez de Balboa in 1513. The first recorded Black freedom fighter to rise against slavery in Panama was King Bayano. Revered and respected among his people, he was feared by the Spanish. His legacy will never be forgotten as he established the first community of free Blacks, called cimarrones, in the Americas (Pike, 2007). Also known as Ballano or Vaino, he was a native African enslaved by the Spanish and is most known for leading the largest slave revolts in Panama during the 16th century (Gallup-Diaz, 2010).

Originally from the Yoruba peoples of West Africa, he led the 1552 revolt against the Spanish colonizers. His troops included hundreds of cimarrones or escaped slaves, who set up freedom colonies known as palenques and consistently fought off the Spanish colonizers and slavers. Their allies included pirates and indigenous peoples. They all faced a common enemy. While the guerilla leader died in a Spanish prison, King Bayano's name lives on today. Other leaders followed him, including Luis de Mozambique (Lavina, 2016).

KING MIGUEL (VENEZUELA) As noted by Dr. Natalia Silva Prada, Ph.D., there was a long line of Black/African kings who formed freedom colonies in resistance to slavery (Prada, 2013). The more one digs, the more one finds. King Miguel or Miguel I of Buria, a contemporary of King Bayano, was born in Puerto Rico and was enslaved in the gold mines in Venezuela. There, he rose in rank. Upon escape, he built a community in Lara, Venezuela around 1552 with his wife as queen and his son as the prince. Regularly, his army attacked Spanish settlements. His kingdom, however short-lived, was known for its order and customs. Miguel died fighting the Spanish in 1555.

GASPAR YANGA (MEXICO) Less than 20 years after King Bayano and King Miguel revolted, another warrior king would emerge. His name was Gaspar Yanga and he led the fight for freedom in 1570. This time, the battleground was in Veracruz, Mexico.

Yanga, who escaped the chains of slavery, was born in 1545 in West Africa. He orchestrated the formation of their own maroon colony in the highlands near Veracruz, Mexico in 1570 and successfully stood off the attacks of the Spanish in 1609 at 64 years of age.

Gaspar Yanga, King Bayano and King Miguel all demonstrated clearly that our ancestors were fighting for freedom from the very first day, and that although their chances of victory were slim, where there is a will, there is a way. Further, they all demonstrated how meaningful freedom colonies were. With a fragile geo-political situation, these warriors seized the moment, hit the opponent where it hurt most, and established their own kingdoms.

ZUMBI (BRASIL) Hollywood has no problem portraying images of Black men as inmates, criminals, hypersexual predators, and absentee dads, but has yet to tell the amazing story of Zumbi (1655 – November 20, 1695) in Brazil. As mentioned earlier, slavery in South America was booming long before here in the US. Further, Brazil ended up with the largest concentration of Blacks outside of Africa. While there are 40 million Blacks in the US, Brazil has about 100 million.

Thus, one can rest assured that warrior kings rose up in Brazil as well. Actually, given the three previous examples, Brazilian freedom colonies were inevitable simply based on the large number of slaves there.

A most famous freedom fighter in Brazil was Zumbi. He was king of the Quilombo dos Palmares, a freedom or maroon colony established by escaped slaves. Although he was killed in the end, he is regarded as a national hero still today for his courage and bravery.

With a 300-year history of slavery going back to 1552, Brazil has a long, dark history of slavery and abuses of human beings (Kent, 2009). Despite all of the money made by Portugal and corporations on the backs of free slave labor, Zumbi's example serves as inspiration for generations yet unborn.

NANNY (JAMAICA) Now, let us not forget that there were warrior queens, too. Nanny the Maroon Queen of Jamaica (c. 1686 – c. 1755) is the most famous. For those who've visited Jamaica, her face is on the $500 bill. Legend has it that as the British soldiers shot their bullets at her, 'she turned around and flipped her backside to them and the bullets ricocheted back and knocked the soldiers down to the ground.' For those who can appreciate the culture and influence of Jamaica on the world, including Reggae music, Marcus Mosiah Garvey, Peter Tosh, and, of course, Robert Nesta "Bob" Marley, then understand that at the root of it all is the Queen: "Queen Nanny" or "Granny Nanny".

Nanny is the 18th-century leader of the Jamaican Maroons. Nanny led a community of formerly enslaved Africans called the Windward Maroons. In the early 18th century, under the leadership of Nanny, the Windward Maroons fought a guerrilla war over many years against

British authorities in the Colony of Jamaica in what became known as the First Maroon War (Campbell, 1990).

Although Blacks are often painted as anything but intelligently fearless leaders with the acumen to lead and to conquer, here we have Bayano fighting in Panama, Miguel battling in Venezuela, and Yanga successfully leading the way in Mexico in 1609 against the Spanish. Zumbi fought ferociously until the bitter end in 1695 against the Portugese in Brasil. And Nanny succeeded by way of treaty with the British – leading to the Maroon's own land in Jamaica in 1740. King Bayano, King Miguel, Gaspar Yanga, Zumbi and Nanny - although super-dynamic in their own regards - set the stage for what was to come next.

These fierce freedom fighters all showed in four different instances that freedom was attainable indeed provided Blacks had the willingness to fight. These heroes demonstrated for those who yearned the taste of freedom that it was one hundred percent possible, especially when people knew their roles and worked cooperatively together. You see, they knew their freedom depended on the strictest level of cohesion. Their lives as well as the lives of their children, grandchildren, and generations to come were dependent on them successfully overcoming any petty differences so as to collectively accomplish the long-held vision of freedom they all so fervently desired.

Further, I submit to you that it is this same type of teamwork and commitment that made Tulsa's Black Wall Street as well as others across the country so successful.

Additionally, each victory provided hope and encouragement for others still enslaved throughout the Americas. As slave revolts occurred and freedom colonies were established, the news spread near and far. Thus, one key lesson is that small victories lead to bigger victories. Also, I am reminded of my late father's words of wisdom: "If you just get out there and try, someone may see you and even help; but you'll never know if you never try." Fortune indeed favors the bold!

TOUSSAINT LOVERTURE (HAITI) Case in point: More than any other Black liberation victory on this side of the world, this historic slave revolt has major financial repercussions still today. The country is Haiti. The European colonizers this time are the French, under the guise of one, Napoleon Bonaparte. The hometown favorite this go-around was a proud Black man named François-Dominique Toussaint Louverture (1743 – April 7, 1803).

Toussaint Louverture, a highly-respected military tactician and formidable opponent, led the Haitian Revolution, the most successful slave insurrection in the history of the modern world (Bell, 2008). He fought against the French, the Spanish and the English and emerged with a victory that shattered the glass ceiling of Western imperialism (James, 1989). News of it inspired people around the globe. To others, it sent a message that slavery and all of its brutality must end immediately.

It let slave owners in other countries understand that at any point, life as they know it could expeditiously come to a turbulent end. It also inspired the enslaved across the Western Hemisphere that despite chains, whips, dogs, and vicious overseers on horseback, freedom and liberation from oppression was very much possible.

Further, history assures us that wherever there existed the burden of slavery, there, too, was an equally and sometimes stronger propensity for freedom. The United States was no exception.

8

Freedom Colonies in the USA

When it comes to the establishment of the United States, let us remember that initially, this included only 13 British colonies along the Eastern seaboard. It was a much smaller nation than it is today. We should also be mindful that a number of European powers had North American interests, too, and that the British were amongst the last to arrive. Simply put, the early American landscape was ever-evolving and involved a number of different players and many moving parts.

With this in mind, know that enslaved Blacks in these British colonies sought freedom just as much as those enslaved elsewhere and were just as willing to fight and/or die for their freedom. And when they did escape, they did the same thing that was done in Venezuela, Panama, Mexico, Haiti and Jamaica: they joined up with our escaped Blacks, Indigenous peoples and any others seeking refuge, including whites.

As it relates to the journey to Indian Territory, let us focus on the southeast part of the country - for this is where we find the first Blacks who paved the way westward to the future home of Tulsa's Black Wall Street.

THE GULLAH ISLANDS

Still unbeknownst to many, the oldest such Black community that fits our definition of a freedom colony in the US is in the Gullah/Geechee Islands, where Black History, as we know it today, goes back to the 1500s when some of the first kidnapped Africans escaped Spanish captors. (Polascak, 2019).

Located off the coast of South Carolina in the Lowcountry, the region spans roughly from Jacksonville, N.C. to Jacksonville, Florida. There are an estimated half-million Blacks in the Gullah Islands today. Those who live off the coast of Georgia are referred to as Geechee. Collectively, the Gullah and the Geechee peoples are well-noted for maintaining much of their African culture, including Creole language and food, over the centuries.

The Gullah and Geechee people did much the same thing that escaped Blacks did elsewhere in the world. As shown in previous examples – from Brazil to Mexico to the Caribbean, escaped Blacks went as deep as possible into the natural habitat, including the mountains, the bush and the swamp. This provided them with cover and protection from those who would put them back in chains.

SOUTH CAROLINA

It is no secret that South Carolina always had a lot of Blacks. Because of its geographic location and significance to the slave trade, South Carolina had a Black majority in the 1700s where Blacks outnumbered whites 2-to-1. This bitter chapter of American history is currently being crystalized as construction is underway for the new International African American Museum in Charleston, set to open in 2022. This is particularly meaningful to me considering my paternal grandfather, Samuel Glover, was from Cordova – 10 minutes from Orangeburg, SC.

Hence, the 1739 Cato Rebellion in Stono, South Carolina should be no surprise. To date, it was the largest slave revolt in a British colony in America. This insurrection had a growing number of escaped Blacks from several plantations who had killed nearly two dozen whites. They were seemingly well on their way to freedom in Spanish Florida, but they ran into strong resistance along the way where those who were not killed were sold back into slavery in the West Indies (Thornton, 1991).

While it was not victorious, it certainly planted a seed of hope to others and nonetheless served as proof positive that the chains of slavery could indeed be broken – even in America.

FLORIDA

Florida, however, is of particular interest to this book because this is where it all happens! History demonstrates how the state is an integral part of the story of the Black man in America, including those in Oklahoma. Florida was initially established by Spain's Ponce De Leon in 1513 and owned by Spain until 1831 when it was purchased by the United States for a sum of $5 million. This is essential because up until then, Spain would offer freedom to ex-slaves from the Southern colonies who made it to Florida. This was made possible by King Charles of Spain's emancipation proclamation, the Edict of 1693. As a result, Blacks escaping slavery in Georgia and the Carolinas would flee to Spanish Florida (Smith, 2018).

In exchange for their freedom, the escaped Blacks agreed to convert to Catholicism and fight for the militia. Spain sold Florida after General Andrew Jackson had invaded it in his Indian Removal efforts. Jackson sought to clear every Native and escaped Black out of Florida by any means necessary. This encroachment led to the three Seminole Wars (1817–18, 1835–42, 1855–58).

Prior to the Jackson onslaught, Fort Mose (or Gracia Real de Santa Teresa de Mose), nearby St. Augustine, and Negro Fort were all early American freedom or maroon colonies. They featured free Blacks, Natives and whites. Increasingly, Florida was more attractive to fugitive slaves as well as various Indigenous peoples collectively referred to as Seminoles (a derivative of the Spanish word cimarrones and used to describe fleeing Natives).

Unfortunately for these peoples, this land was also attractive to white settlers. These whites, some of whom had slaves, were clearly uncomfortable living near free armed Blacks. It is not difficult to understand what unfolded in the years to come. Blacks were fleeing to Florida. Native Americans were being pushed out of colonial areas and consequently moved to Florida. And then came the white settlers. And that's when the insidious bravado of Gen. Jackson was on full display. He was America's white knight.

It was fascinating to learn that Florida, the same state where George Zimmerman stalked and killed Trayvon Martin and who hid behind the "Stand Your Ground Law" in 2012, was also the site of such key developments in early America involving Blacks. These events ultimately helped shape the destiny of this country. Learning about this history gave me a new favorable perspective on Florida. Initially, after the Zimmerman trial, I swore to never go to Florida again.

9

Blacks, Indians and Whites

BLACKS, INDIANS AND WHITES

For the purposes of this book and its focus on the Greenwood District of Tulsa, Oklahoma, there is one significant slave insurrection that is totally ignored in American history texts as if it were a deadly disease. It has been conveniently revised and tucked away right under our noses. It featured possibly the bravest Black man ever.

Many of us have heard about the Seminole Wars in Florida. They were the result of the Indian Removal Act designed to push Indians off of their valuable and fertile lands for the sake of white settlers and usher these Indigenous peoples westward to Indian Territory. This land to the west would eventually become known as the State of Oklahoma. What was *not* taught is that the Second Seminole War (1835-1842) was both the largest and the most successful slave insurrection in the history of the United States.

The US colonists were not just battling the Seminoles, but escaped Blacks – or Maroons, as well. This changes the complexion of the situation in a way not typically discussed.

Let me just add that until researching for this book, Gabriel Prosser, Nat Turner and Denmark Vesey were the main Black American insurrectionists with which this writer was most familiar. I did not realize that slave insurrections were more common. Many thanks to Dr. Eugenia Collier for exposing me to the topic some 25 years ago at Morgan State University.

Today, I now have an even clearer understanding of how things really went down. Contrary to the storylines shoved onto society by Hollywood and the mainstream media, history shows that Blacks have been fighting against enslavement from the very beginning, and despite many, many losses, have on occasion emerged victoriously. Who Knew?

2nd SEMINOLE WAR & CHIEF JOHN HORSE

According to the traditional version, the three Seminole Wars were conflicts between the US Government and the Seminole Indians in Spanish Florida beginning in 1817 and ending in 1858. That is the official description.

Note that there is no reference to Blacks whatsoever.

Now, remember, it was previously noted that Florida was a Spanish colony and the preferred destination for many Blacks escaping slavery in the South, thanks to the Spanish. Yet, the storyline perpetuated in the American educational system consistently fails to credit Blacks with almost any successful armed resistance to slavery – beyond the 1997 movie "Amistad" which focused on the 1839 overthrow of the ship off the coast of Cuba.

The truth is, though, that Chief John Horse is that authentic American icon this nation has been longing to remember, for he is quite possibly the greatest Black commander in American history. I only wish I had learned about him and what he did from Florida to Mexico a long time ago.

John Horse was the modern-day equivalent of a John Wick, John Wayne and Captain James T. Kirk of "Star Trek" all rolled into one. Or, one could say he had his own "Wakanda" in full-effect. However, it's framed, he was the indomitable one, that leader who would show the rest of us how to win – how to make the impossible happen.

He and other Blacks fought boldly beside the Seminoles in the 2nd Seminole War (December 23, 1835 – August 14, 1842) against the colonizing encroachers in Florida who wanted to take their land and who wanted back those Blacks who had escaped slavery (Porter, 2013).

It should be noted that Prof. Kenneth W. Porter was the leading authority on John Horse and his book, *The Black Seminoles: History of a Freedom-Seeking People*, includes interviews with Horse's descendants and acquaintances who provided the author with first-hand accounts back in the 1940s and 50s. I am confident that this kind of liberating Black history was no more popular then as it is now. Still, Porter led the way in shining light on Chief Horse, including his body of work beyond Oklahoma.

To end the 2nd Seminole War, Horse negotiated a truce where he agreed to lead his people across the Mississippi into Indian Territory where they were promised freedom by the US government (May, 2009). It is important to know that some Seminoles disagreed with his decision to stop fighting, putting his life in continual danger among former allies.

Upon arrival in Indian Territory, Horse learned that US government reneged on their promise of freedom. He then led some 200 Black families to Nacimiento, Mexico where he and his troops were hired by the Mexican government as the border patrol for northern Mexico. Then, Mexico essentially reneged on him or, put differently, subjected them to some unnecessary red tape. Whatever the case, he then led a group back to Texas after the Civil War.

By the way, there still hails a community of Black Mexicans today in Nacimiento and they proudly celebrate their Blackness every year during Juneteenth. Furthermore, some of those soldiers and their descendants even went on to serve as Seminole Scouts for the US military. Nonetheless, Chief John Horse is the greatest American hero I've ever heard of in my life. Some refer to him as the "Moses" of Oklahoma.

Chief John Horse led more Blacks to war against the American government than any other uprising in American history. He fought with over twelve hundred other Blacks and Indians against those, like Andrew Jackson, who were insistent on ridding Florida of both Blacks and Indians. These whites wanted the Indians dead or gone and they wanted Blacks in chains. As a matter of fact, Jackson became a hero in America's eyes for this great American attempt at genocide. The goal was to remove these people to Indian Territory in what was later called Oklahoma. This long and brutal trek, known as the Trail of Tears, saw thousands die from the ferocious cold, hunger, and disease. Through it all, including assassination attempts on his life, Chief Horse prevailed as a very powerful leader (Porter, 1947).

According to Amy Sturgis, Ph.D. of Lenoir-Rhyne University, Horse led his people right into the annals of history: "They created the largest haven in the US South for runaway slaves, they led the largest slave revolt in US history, they secured the only emancipation of rebellious slaves prior to the Civil War, and they formed the largest mass exodus of slaves across the United States moving from the Florida Everglades through Indian Territory - what would become Oklahoma - eventually locating in Mexico where they secured title to their own land. It's a remarkable story. It's part-'Spartacus' and part-'Braveheart' and part-'Amistad' and part-'Glory' with a little bit of 'Dances with Wolves' thrown in, a story decades long of oppression and freedom fighting. I don't understand why there hasn't been more attention given to John Horse and the Black Seminoles (Sturgis, 2012)."

What is remarkable about American history is that it is full of stories of slavery, yet the story of Blacks rebuking this wicked institution is rarely ever discussed. If ever there was a story about the will and determination of a people to be free, it is the story of these warriors in Florida. Truthfully, before doing the research for this book, I had never heard of Chief Horse. Now, I know how gripping his story is and why it must be shared.

This Archdiocese of Baltimore account sheds even more insight on this legendary man's tenure post-Florida:

"The arrival in Indian Territory (Oklahoma) was more dangerous than living in Florida. This was Creek Indian Territory. Creeks had settled on the land the Army had promised to the Seminoles but the Creeks were notorious for capturing, selling and enslaving blacks. During John's next trip to Washington, D.C., he lobbied for but was unable to secure a treaty to receive separate land, however he was granted property at Fort Gibson. While he was in Washington, then Attorney General John Mason ruled that the Black Seminoles were functionally fair game for slave raiders. John returned to find his sister's children had been captured by the Creeks and sold. The children were lost forever. Upon his return John and Chief Wildcat led all the Seminoles to Wewoka, Oklahoma with the possibility of an alliance with other tribes. This was Cherokee region. In 1849, John and Chief Wildcat led their people across Texas and the Rio Grande River and into Coahuila, Mexico. On July 12, 1850, they presented themselves at Piedra Negras and were given land in Mexico for settlement. He fought in the Mexico Army riding his horse 'American', and was given the rank of colonel. When the Civil War ended, John returned to the United States along with many of the Black Indians and settled near Fort Duncan, Texas, where he remained until the summer of 1876. His final days were spent negotiating for promised land for Black Indians. But the fourth assassination attempt on his life left him severely wounded. John Horse returned to Mexico to secure land grants near Nacimiento. God called him home before he reached Mexico City whispering 'a job well done' (Porter-Mitchell, 2012)."

Through all of this, Chief John Horse was simply, miraculously, and magnificently astounding! He and his Seminole army are part of the answer, if you ask me, to the age-old question of how the West was won. Even more, they pioneered Black progress in the West, created their own role in the US armed forces, set the example for Black excellence, and constructed Black towns along the way to and in Oklahoma, Texas, and Mexico (Mulroy, 2017).

I want people to know that there is a long tradition of Black freedom fighters in the Americas. Know that our ancestors did not simply cower and accept slavery as their destiny. Instead, a warrior king or queen almost always rose to the occasion. The list of notables includes King Miguel in Venezuela; King Bayano in Panama; Gaspar Yanga in Mexico; Zumbi in Brazil; Nanny in Jamaica; and Toussaint Loverture in Haiti.

These gladiators fought gallantly for their freedom. And for those who did gain their freedom, the next step was setting up maroon colonies or towns, which is the very foundation of a Black Wall Street.

Hence, Greenwood and the rest of Oklahoma, were birthed out of a relentless liberation effort by the likes of people like Seminole Chief John Horse. Although his trek went all the way to Mexico, his era signifies the first wave of Blacks to Oklahoma.

Today, Mexico still remembers this little piece of history: "Although few black people remain in northern Mexico, the region was once home to thousands who escaped slavery in the United States. Mexico outlawed slavery in 1829, an underlying factor in Texas's declaration of independence seven years later. In 1836, there were an estimated 5,000 slaves in Texas, a number that ballooned by 1860 to 182,500—more than 30 percent of the state's population (Ferguson, 2019)."

Horse and his people had pierced the Western frontier all the way to Mexico, building towns along the way. By leading the way to freedom, he was like Moses to his people – a people who literally fought their way free. Now, that is truly a Black Wall Street state-of-mind.

There are so many important lessons one could pull from Chief Horse. For one, a leader is sometimes forced to make his own decision. And sometimes, that decision is unpopular. Keep going anyway! The Seminoles wanted Horse and his soldiers to stay and fight. They are known today as "The Unconquered". But Horse left and went to Oklahoma. And when Oklahoma didn't feel right, he went to Mexico. Sometimes, you may have to change locations. It's that simple.

One place may not be working, even to the point where you think about quitting. You may just need to move. Maybe it's not for you where you are. Maybe, you are meant to be somewhere else. So, try another spot; but whatever you do, don't give up. Keep going! The most important thing is to stay in the game. As a wise man, Ed Hooks, said to me many moons ago, "If you're still thinking, you're still in the game." Those words have served me well over the years.

SECOND WAVE TO OKLAHOMA

Understanding how the second wave of Blacks came into Oklahoma is more complicated. About a decade after Horse and his people entered Oklahoma around 1843, a whole new mass of Blacks would begin to fixate on Kansas. After all, the country was divided over slavery and the Civil War was soon to begin. Further, more settlers were looking beyond the Mississippi for new land to own.

The mindset of many was "Go, West, young man!" This phrase, coined by newsman and author Horace Greeley, is often associated with Manifest Destiny, the white colonists' belief that conquering America was their right (Shane, 2009). Further, anyone, especially those of the darker hue, who got in the way would be killed or enslaved.

Captain John Brown, the noted white abolitionist, had his own set of values and saw things quite differently. A man of God, Brown had just come on the national scene in Kansas around 1855 to join his two sons. He was adamantly opposed to the horrid institution of slavery, and he let it be known.

During this period, with the country clearly headed for Civil War, critical legislation was proposed. Some were for slavery while others were for abolition. For every step towards progress, there was some piece of legislation pushing the pendulum the other way. Specifically, passage of the Kansas-Nebraksa Act in 1854 stoked national tensions regarding slavery because it repealed the Missouri Compromise.

At this time, slavery was the paramount issue of the day. So, any new state seeking to join the United States was fair game for both sides. In short, the two opposing groups were the Free-Staters, anti-slavery settlers who wanted Kansas to be a free state, and the Border Ruffians, pro-slavery settlers. This period between 1855 and 1861, referred to as "Bleeding Kansas," saw matters escalate into armed conflicts. The political climate was extremely ugly.

On May 21, 1856, some proslavery men went into the Free State Hotel in Lawrence, Kansas, set it on fire, burned two printing presses and ransacked the town. In response, Brown led an attack at Pottawatomie Creek.

John Brown is absolutely, unequivocally my favorite white man in history. He and his soldiers made it crystal clear that slavery was not an option in Kansas. And they had no problem killing anyone who tried to stop them. Brown's anti-slavery efforts inspired many in the Deep South. Word spread rapidly that John Brown was fighting to help rid Kansas of slavery and slave owners. Blacks, heavily focused on fleeing the intolerable and inhumane ways of the Deep South, were increasingly eyeing the promised land west of the Mississippi River.

Because of Brown, Kansas became extremely attractive to Southern Blacks. Yes, they would be leaving behind America's most fertile land in the southeast, but in exchange, at least they would be free – or so they thought. They figured moving westward would remove them from the violence and terror they were subjected to living in Southern states.

As the last of John Brown's anti-slavery efforts ended in an attempted raid on the federal armory at Harpers Ferry, Virginia (today West Virginia) in 1859, John Brown became a Northern martyr revered across the land (Bordewich, 2009).

Two years after Brown was killed, the Civil War would finally begin and last until 1865. Slavery had been abolished and the enslaved were freed. What followed was Reconstruction. This era, marked by some 2,000 Blacks being elected to office, would last until the 1877 Compromise which tragically resulted in Union troops being pulled from Southern cities and towns. This era would also see the birth of domestic terrorism in the form of the Ku Klux Klan in Pulaski, Tennessee on Christmas Day in 1865. Other violent white paramilitary terrorist groups and organizations also formed, including the White League (or the White Man's League) founded in 1874 in Grant Parish, Louisiana. And their key political ally was the Democratic Party. This is the cunning nature and the diabolical roots of modern-day institutional racism extending to the highest levels of American government.

Some critical pieces of legislation would go into law. Again, some good and some bad. For instance, the Civil Rights Bill of 1866 was good. The Dred Scott Decision of 1857 and the Black Codes of

1865-66, on the other hand, were pure evil, divisive and ultimately cat-alyzed a massive exodus of Blacks from Southern states heading west-ward. This mass exodus was partly fueled by the New Orleans Massacre and the Memphis Massacre, both in 1866.

One key piece of legislation to this story actually never made it into law, but it certainly planted a seed in the minds of tens of thousands. Rep. William Lawrence of Ohio's 4th District introduced legislation in 1867 proposing territory where all territorial officers and voters would have been black. History suggests, despite never becoming a law, it cer-tainly set the tone for what was to come (Krehbiel, 2020).

Thus, these are some of the roots of thought when it comes to Okla-homa becoming an all-Black state. Couple that with the fact that John Brown's abolition campaign left an ongoing impression in the souls of many, and one should easily see how both Kansas and Oklahoma were viewed as prime destinations for Blacks fleeing Southern oppression.

Lastly, there are three more Black legends who are unsung heroes in this story: Henry Adams of Louisiana, Benjamin "Pap" Singleton of Tennessee, and Robert Reed Church, also of Tennessee. These were ex-ceptional men of vision and courage who, unlike many today, insisted on helping the Black masses find their own place. In those days, there were a number of emigration efforts to send Blacks to Liberia. Nation-ally, emigration efforts took place, too. Henry Adams, for instance, was a big proponent of sending Blacks from the Deep South to Liberia, and that he did for a while. Inspired by the headway made by "Pap" Single-ton and others, he then re-directed his efforts towards helping Blacks get to Kansas.

While John Brown's previous efforts had already given many Blacks hope that Kansas was a good place, that's where "Pap" Singleton, an escaped slave who went North but then returned to Tennessee after the Civil War, took the ball and ran with it. He became the noted leader of this Exoduster Movement to Kansas. On Pap's watch, some 50-70,000 freedmen would seek refuge in Kansas from Louisiana, Mis-sissippi, Texas and Tennessee (Painter, 1990).

Needless to say, it wasn't long before Kansas became oversaturated. Indian Territory, now referred to as the Territory of Oklahoma, just to the south, became a viable option in the minds of some of these refugees. Oklahoma Territory was being touted by the likes of E. P. McCabe as an even better place for Blacks, and possibly even the first Black state. And let us not forget that Chief John Horse had already made an impression there in 1843.

Back in Memphis, a huge benefactor would give the Oklahoma idea a tremendous boost. His name is Robert Reed Church (Wills, 2018). He, too, played a key role in helping Blacks flee the Deep South. Reed, the wealthiest Black man in the South and a noted supporter of journalist Ida B. Wells, used $10,000 (over a quarter-million dollars today) of his own money to help send Blacks not to Kansas, but to Oklahoma. And this would help spark a second wave of Blacks into what is now Oklahoma.

Some of the first all-Black towns included Lincoln City, Langston – where E. P. McCabe made an impression, Brooksville, and Boley, made famous for thwarting a robbery by the Pretty Boy Floyd Gang.

As it relates to Lincoln City, of note is how its first inhabitants included Blacks from Kansas. Also noteworthy is how dedicated these people were to changing their lives for the better. To move one's family and all of one's belongings to a new place loaded with uncertainty was simply audacious and represented entrepreneurship in its truest sense. They risked it all!

Although Lincoln City did not last long, it signified a new beginning. It helped to lay the foundation for future progress. It gave Black America a taste of possibility. It is also a solemn reminder that success does not always come quickly nor on the first try. At the same time, when opportunity does arrive, we must be prepared to take advantage of it. Even more, we must have the vision to be able to foresee the possibilities.

Lincoln City was not a failure because it demonstrated that Blacks could run their own town, just like their white counterparts. I imagine that gave an incredible sense of empowerment to these people. I also imagine how such a sense of empowerment was infectious.

LANGSTON, BOLEY & OTHER BLACK TOWNS

Also of significance to Black History in Oklahoma is a town called Langston for it is where a Black university is established and where we learn more about another great Black visionary.

What, or should I say who, is important to remember here is the legendary visionary himself, E. P. McCabe. While Rev. Carter introduced me to one of Greenwood's Founding Fathers, O. W. Gurley, McCabe was also a dynamo himself. From what I have read, he was as unapologetically Black as they come and only wanted the best for Black people in Oklahoma. To boot, he was a leading advocate for Oklahoma to become the first Black state. Imagine that! Remember, Rep. Lawrence planted legislative seeds for a place for Black people in 1866.

At this point, one should have a keener sense of just how serious Black Oklahomans were. Lincoln City, Langston and Brooksville all speak to the level of commitment these people had to making something out of this place called Oklahoma Territory. And these all-Black towns – at least 50 and as many as 70 altogether - gave people the opportunity to showcase their various skill sets. Further, these towns demonstrated that despite the obvious cultural differences - Blacks, Indians and whites could work together. Better yet, they could fight together, too.

While Tulsa is most-widely known in Black Oklahoma history because of Greenwood's Black Wall Street, there is at least one other town that deserves mention. And that's Boley. Please know that Boley has quite a phenomenal story of its own. Further, I learned that it is virtually impossible to discuss Black Oklahoma without mentioning Boley. And it is impossible to mention Boley without referencing Abigail Vivian Barnett McCormick. McCormick, who was a descendant of the Creek Nation, used her Creek inheritance to establish Boley.

In all, there were as many as 70 all-Black towns in Oklahoma. Neighboring Texas has to be mentioned as well. Of the 4 million newly freed Blacks, one professor suggests that at least one in four of those people set out to build all-Black towns, including in Texas. Professor Andrea Roberts, assistant professor of urban planning in the College of Architecture at Texas A&M University, "has found more than 550 freedom colonies established by the almost 200,000 newly freed African-Americans living in Texas just after the abolition of slavery (Watts, 2018)."

I should note here that today, the Dallas Black Chamber of Commerce is revered as the oldest Black chamber in the nation. This is but a testament to the diligent efforts made by Blacks over the years there in Texas.

The broader significance here is that the 4 million Black people fresh out of slavery had a deep thirst and a hunger for their own, just like those before them who were able to break free. Our strong, Black ancestors took their grit, grind and hustle and put it all together and made bricks for buildings. And these buildings came to become towns. And these towns had businesses. And that's Black Wall Street.

Today, it means using our Smartphones, but it's the same concept. At this juncture, every Black person in America ought to know that we ought to be building relationships and doing business far beyond our zip codes. Today, Black Wall Street is global. You can send an email to Nigeria just as fast as you can send one downtown. Just do it!

It is time that we use these digital resources and everything else at our disposal for the sake of building legacy wealth we can pass on to our children. The time is now. Do it and do it now!

10

CONCLUSION

Tho' much is taken, much abides; and tho'
We are not now that strength which in old days
Moved earth and heaven, that which we are, we are;
One equal temper of heroic hearts,
Made weak by time and fate, but strong in will
To strive, to seek, to find, and not to yield.
- Tennyson

So, who knew this information? I sure as heck didn't.

It is my hope that you, too, are inspired by these findings to go out and learn more of these untold nuggets of Black history. I also hope that the reader is inspired to become more business-minded in all of one's affairs – especially in light of the COVID-10 pandemic. After all, these Black people made daring moves, established their own towns and even created profitable ventures in the 1800s without the benefits of modern-day society. Today, we have computers, iPads, and laptops. I am only suggesting that we play to our strengths and use the available technology to better secure our fiscal future, especially in the realm of business.

My summation begs the question – what does all of this mean?

For me, this incredible history is a steady reminder that we stand on the shoulders of some pretty phenomenal ancestors. To have endured what they did and yet persevered in countless instances is simply supernatural. They had every excuse in the world to quit, but instead they forged ahead and built Black towns, including hundreds in East Texas. From Eatonville, Florida – one of the first self-governing all-Black municipalities in the United States founded in 1887 and made famous by Zora Neale Hurston to Mound Bayou, Mississippi (also established in 1887) to Allensworth, California, the first town in California established exclusively by a group of Blacks in 1908 led by Col. Allen Allensworth, the US Army's highest ranking Black officer in 1906 – Black people have always been on a mission to establish our own.

And please, let's not forget about New York City. Two of the oldest Black communities are in this metropolis. As slavery was abolished by 1804 in the Northern states, Seneca Village would emerge in Manhattan (between 82nd and 89th, what is now Central Park) in 1825 and Weeksville would develop in Brooklyn between what is now Bedford-Stuyvesant and Crown Heights in 1835. The Weeksville Heritage Center at 158 Buffalo Avenue today serves as a constant reminder to yet another amazing piece of Black history right before our very eyes. Seneca Village and Weeksville are proof positive of what Blacks accomplished in the early 1800s. Although this might be unfathomable to us today, especially given the political climate in America at the time, but it doesn't change what happened.

Wherever there were Black people, rest assured there was some kind of Black business district or Black Wall Street. Mostly all of these Black communities had some place where Blacks came together. And while most of these communities were relatively modest in size, let it also be noted that Chicago was founded by a Black furrier, Jean Baptiste Point du Sable, in the 1780s.

Black people never took slavery lying down. There have always been Black freedom fighters who denounced servitude and who fought to destroy it: King Miguel in Venezuela; King Bayano in Panama; Gaspar Yanga in Veracruz, Mexico; Zumbi in Brazil; Queen Nanny in Jamaica; General Toussaint in Haiti; and Chief John Horse in America.

And there is one white man above all others who truly showed his love for God and man: Captain John Brown, the abolitionist who died fighting the good fight.

Further, let it be known that Black people were far more involved in the building of this country than American history gives credit. America's films, from the very beginning, have attempted to belittle the contributions of our regal Black ancestors and relegate them as mere servants. That's why we need more film producers like Spike Lee who know our history; Lee understands that he stands on the shoulders of the pioneering Oscar Micheaux (1884-1951), who created 44 films in his lifetime. This is how we counter the racist chicanery of a D. W. Griffith: With light!

This is why we must know about James Forten, the free Black patriot who fought in the Revolutionary War and who was also owned a very successful sail business in Philadelphia. Forten was also an abolitionist who helped fund the Underground Railroad and used more than half of his wealth to purchase the freedom of slaves (Winch, 2002). This man, like a few others in history, truly exemplified the meaning of Black Wall Street in how he lived and how he looked out for others, including white employees who tended to vote in the direction he saw fit. He was a Black Wall Street all by himself. In terms of being a patriot, he was actually opposed to emigration efforts to send Blacks back to Africa. He believed he was entitled to as much as anyone else in this country and lived his life accordingly. Further, like E. P. McCabe in Oklahoma, like Chief John Horse, like so many other leaders in history – not everyone is going to understand one's decisions. Sometimes, the leader makes an unpopular decision that actually gets greater than expected outcomes. A lesson is this: If there is no path, pave a way!

There is not enough mention of free Black patriots like Agrippa Hull from Southampton, Massachusetts, who served for 6 years in the Revolutionary War or of prominent Philadelphian Octavius Valentine Catto, who was an activist, scholar, athlete, and military officer during the Civil War. Some of us know about these and other soldiers of that era, but we never talk much about Blacks who were free at the time. They did, in fact, live and even contribute to the cause of freeing other Black people. This is why we can never, ever forget our Black soldiers, male and female. For one, fighting in uniform usually meant an end to slavery for the soldier (if he were not already free). Secondly, each time that soldier went off to war and returned home, his presence automatically liberated those around him. After returning from war, this soldier's return made everybody stand a little taller. I'd need another whole book to just begin to explain how significant the Black soldier is in all of our Black progress from the start.

Nonetheless, my people have been starved of this information about the greatness of our ancestors for far too long. It is time for these stories to go viral.

The January 6, 2021 assault on the Capitol Building was a stark reminder that the same mentality that thought it was okay to enslave people before the Civil War is unfortunately still alive today. And they are armed.

However, despite these violent, racist terrorists, despite the redlining, despite the challenges with gaining credit and access to capital, there is a whole new generation of highly-motivated Black entrepreneurs in play and they are not shy or tepid. They are audaciously optimistic and eager to learn, in my honest opinion.

Not a day goes by on social media where a new Black business isn't being announced. Even in a pandemic. Yes! There is a new battalion of strong, youthful entrepreneurs who find inspiration in a Nipsey Hussle, a Killer Mike in Atlanta with his new bank, a Terence Dickson of Terra Café Bmore and Terra Loft Consulting in Baltimore, and a slew of people of which I have never even heard. Increasingly, more Black people are taking up the reins of entrepreneurship, buying back blocks and rehabbing houses like never before.

This dynamic generation insists that where there is no way, they will carve out a path. They believe that if Chief John Horse could fight against slavery, negotiate a truce and land, and then move to Mexico to do it all again, then they can damn sure go down to the state building and register a business name, get an EIN, open a business bank account, get a Dunn & Bradstreet number, and land a federal contract – thanks to the efforts of people like the late Maryland Congressman Parren J. Mitchell who helped create the federal 8(a) program in 1987 (Logan, 1977). Many agree that because of Mitchell's advocacy back then, and with the help of Pres. Jimmy Carter, the 8(a) program has produced generations of Black millionaires since (Xion, 2020).

Of this new cadre of entrepreneurs rising, it should be reiterated continuously that the most tenacious of them all is the Black woman. Her credit is good. Her debt is down. She's done blowing money on shopping and now investing in BITCOIN, real estate investment trusts and the stock market.

And, if she isn't running her own business, she is now running a Fortune 500. Kudos to Rosalind Brewer, the Black woman who was CEO of Walgreens Boots Alliance and Sam's Club; she is now COO of Starbucks – the first woman and the first Black to do so. How's that for destroying glass ceilings?

A recent *Forbes* article reminds, "Black women represent 42% of new women-owned businesses—three times their share of the female population—and 36% of all Black-owned employer businesses. High levels of educational attainment, coupled with overcoming barriers to corporate advancement, have prompted Black women to pursue entrepreneurship, where they've become a potent economic force. Majority Black women-owned firms grew 67% from 2007 to 2012, compared to 27% for all women, and 50% from 2014 to 2019, representing the highest growth rate of any female demographic during that time frame (Umoh, 2020)."

Like the rapper Drake, I, too, have high hopes! I see a new day for America's Black business owners. I see increasing collaboration with African nations, like Jamal Adkins from East Baltimore. This brother moved to Zambia with his wife and has established a growing enterprise. Such a feat would make the late Rev. Leon Sullivan extremely proud. After all, Africa is the future. But, too, that's another book. For now, each of us must do our part in supporting Black businesses, no matter what. As a matter of fact, I need you to make the pledge:

"I, (your name), promise to support Black businesses wherever and whenever I can, as often as possible, no matter what. I don't have to love the owner. I don't even have to like them. However, if they are providing a viable product or service and are employing Black people, than I have an innate responsibility to support them. I AM BLACK WALL STREET!"

I pray that this book is a solemn reminder that freedom ain't free. If it's Black and in America, best believe that somewhere, somehow, somebody fought, bled and may have even died fighting for the opportunity a long time ago. Therefore, it is incumbent upon us today to take full advantage of the technology, wisdom, institutional knowledge, and other empowering resources readily available to us via the nearest cellphone. We should not allow any excuses whatsoever to deter us from what we can and should accomplish, including creating and growing some of the most dynamic and successful businesses in America. The playing field is more level than ever before. And although that is not saying a lot, especially given America's history of slavery and racism, it is imperative that we do everything within our power to maximize the access we do have.

The American landscape is changing every single day. The nation of our birth is becoming increasingly diverse and multi-cultural. The time is now for us to accentuate our positives and capitalize on the market in the most effective manner possible. Ultimately, it means creating services and manufacturing products that all people will need and buy. But of course, charity starts at home. So, it would be ideal if we all deliberately make a goal to spend more with Black-owned businesses. That's only common sense!

And that's a critical lesson we must never forget. Our ancestors, fresh out of slavery, saved their pennies, nickels and quarters to help build towns, churches, Black Wall Streets, and some of our first Historically Black Colleges and Universities. Today, however, with all our advanced degrees, six-figure salaries, homes with picket fences, and luxury rides outside our doors, we are witnessing the closing of the very institutions that propelled us to where we are today. Something is fundamentally wrong with this scenario.

And that is exactly why a Deion Sanders using all his influence to help contribute to the football program at Jackson State is so meaningful. Eddie George, the Heisman Trophy winner, is now coaching at Tennessee State. Both schools are HBCUs. That is also why seeing a Lebron James build schools and businesses that impact Black youth and adults is so on-point. And I can't leave out Magic Johnson. I am so proud of his business mindedness and his lasting commitment to help empower other Blacks, including those in our inner-cities.

Let's all put our energy now into supporting Black business owners across America and beyond. Remember, we don't have to be in love with somebody to support their Black business. We don't even have to like them. However, if they are employing Black people in a constructive way, then it shouldn't even matter. I am ever-mindful of how Annie Malone and Madam C.J. Walker showed Black women how to take care of their hair, created products, and mentored others. Black women, in essence, created the Black beauty industry. Sadly, today, we are witnessing others make billions annually off it. I don't think I'll ever be able to fully-accept how we went from being top producers to top consumers.

That is exactly why the lessons of those early freedom fighters cannot be forsaken. I'm sure there was inner-turmoil within the first freedom colonies. I'm sure there were power struggles. However, like the enemy we fight, we must be organized. We have to put our petty differences aside and focus on the common issue at hand: Better controlling our dollars and supporting Black businesses.

This time around, though, the fight is not with weapons. For today's fight, we need our brightest legal minds, like Attorney Damario Solomon Simmons in Tulsa and Attorney J. Wyndal Gordon in Baltimore, pushing the envelope in the courts. We need our most brilliant engineers to invent and create products that can revolutionize healthy living. And we need all our Wall Street banking and finance types to use their business acumen to catapult these newly emerging firms to going public.

We also need more elected officials, like Maryland's Black Republican Lt. Gov. Boyd Rutherford and state Senator Antonio Hayes, who understand the significance of assisting a business like Citywide Youth Development in obtaining funding for their new $3 million manufacturing plant. We need more Republicans, like Rutherford, and more Democrats, like Hayes, who understand William Clay's famous line: "This is quite a game, politics. There are no permanent enemies, and no permanent friends, only permanent interests" (Clay, 2000).

We need more Marion Barrys, Maynard Jacksons, and Parren J. Mitchells. We need Black leaders who understand that if the politics do not translate into economics, then we have collectively failed. I challenge every reader to get the phone number of every local, state, and federal elected official representing them; and then, contact them, engage them, and finding out what they are working on at the present. Remember, it's all about relationships – just like with the banks. We have to build relationships that matter.

We also need the everyday person to play their role. To truly transform Black America, it's about where we spend our money. This includes every Black man, woman, and child. I need each one of us to proudly proclaim to the world: I AM BLACK WALL STREET!

If we make a deliberate attempt to buy Black no matter what, we can help these businesses hire people who look like us. After all, the best crime plan in the world is a j-o-b. A working person is too busy focused on the job than to be wasting time getting into trouble. We all know that an idle mind is the devil's workshop.

There is no need to get angry about non-Blacks setting up shop in our community. Instead, focus on buying and growing our own. That is the true spirit of Black Wall Street. In DC, New York, Atlanta, Oakland – wherever. And with so much online, we really have no excuse. Truth be told, if we don't support each other, then we are committing economic suicide ... to the tune of nearly $2 trillion in annual disposable income. Do the math! (Others have!)

The fight for freedom and equity is still very much in play, but for this battle we will need a sound mind and a righteous spirit. These moral and spiritual attributes will fortify us and help us succeed – along with an impeccable work ethic and an invincible determination that growls back louder than the doubt in the mirror and boldly proclaims, "I Am Black Wall Street"!

Meanwhile, wishing the best for the group represented by Tulsa Attorney Simmons and their current lawsuit on behalf of the victims and the descendants of the Tulsa Massacre. Neither the people of Greenwood District nor their descendants have ever been compensated. Now seems like as good a time as any to ameliorate the transgressions of the past, especially if it is within one's power. Why wouldn't they, you know?

Lastly, I have a word for the Black business owners in my hometown, Baltimore. Baltimore has a long, rich legacy of Black Excellence. Harriet Tubman and Frederick Douglass spent time here; as did W. E. B. Du Bois. Benjamin Banneker, the great engineer, hailed out of Baltimore County. Joseph Locks Funeral Home, established in 1835 in East Baltimore, is one of - if not the oldest Black family business in America. Owned today by my late father's colleague, Cynthia Galmor, I speak with her often of the value of that history and of the need to preserve that history. Isaac Myers was also in East Baltimore. He ran a ship caulkers union for Black laborers in Baltimore on the waterfront to ensure Blacks got fair wages. Interestingly, Frederick Douglass did a stint as the leader there, too. Supreme Court Justice Thurgood Marshall was born and raised in Baltimore. Giants like Thomas Smith, owner of the Smith Hotel at the turn of the 20th century, laid the groundwork for our business success a long time ago. Smith, the largest Black hotelier in the United States at the time, obliterated the stereotypes put forth about Blacks by mainstream media. He was most enterprising, very political, and he understood power. He commanded respect. After him, another iconic figure took the scene. His name was Little Willie Adams. His wife, Victorine, was the first Black woman to serve on the Baltimore City Council. Like Smith, Adams understood money and power and single-handedly financed several Black businesses with his street lottery business. He also, like Smith, financially supported politicians.

The point is that succeeding in business is nothing new to us. We've always figured out how to navigate the game. Despite the obstacles, the game has never been new to us. One learns and then passes it on to the next generation. Then comes a Reginald F. Lewis, the Black man who orchestrated the $1 billion corporate takeover of TLC Beatrice in 1987. How's that for Black Wall Street?

And the list goes on: Henry Parks and Raymond V. Haysbert, Sr. They *were* Black Wall Street. Robert Lee "Bob" Clay: He was Black Wall Street. Arnold Jolivet, Esq.: He was most assuredly Black Wall Street. Councilman Kenny Harris: He, too, was Black Wall Street.

We all stand on colossal shoulders, and we can never forget the sacrifices of those who proudly came before us. Further, we must teach these lessons to our children as our future depends on their ability to apply them to their own lifetime. Like a well-oiled 4x400m relay team, we must seamlessly pass the baton to the next generation of leaders ... in real time – without a hitch.

As for me, I am going to continue to be an advocate for Black business through *BmoreNews.com* and *BlackUSA.News*. I am going to continue to push the envelope on our behalf, and raise pertinent business questions to the local, state and federal political candidates I encounter. And I am going to continue to work with Ron Busby at the US Black Chamber. I am going to continue to build a bridge with the members of the Black Business Empowerment Commission based in Harlem, including Walter Edwards (the modern day Godfather of Harlem), Regina Smith of the Harlem Business Alliance, architect Zevilla Preston Jackson, and youthful brand builder Tasemere Gathers. And I will work even more with the members of the nation's top Black chamber, the Oakland African American Chamber of Commerce, including Cathy Adams, Tammy Willis, and Doug Blacksher. Furthermore, I am working with leading Black business advocate Tamara Brown to connect with Boston's Black business advocacy efforts. Recently, BECMA (Black Economic Council of Massachusetts) and other groups filed a lawsuit against the city of Boston for consistently blocking minorities from getting business (Cotter, 2021). Mind you, Blacks are discriminated against across the country, but when a group like BECMA steps out there ... in Boston, then it is our job to support them by any means necessary.

Thank you to all of the people who have supported us over the years, including our Joe Manns Black Wall Street Awards. To further this cause and formalize our efforts, we have formed a non-profit: National Black Wall Street Foundation, 1142 N. Carrollton Avenue, Baltimore, MD 21217, USA.

We welcome your support.

Prayerfully, in the next 10 years, we can honor another 1,700 entrepreneurs, if not more. And we will continue to connect businesses with the resources and technical assistance they need to get to the next level, including media exposure.

And don't forget to support the Black Press by advertising your business and events. Our news outlets are *BmoreNews.com, the news before the news,* and *BlackUSA.News, the voice of our people.* We specialize in covering the Black experience. Without you, there is no us! For marketing, advertising or speaking engagements, please call **DMGlobal Marketing & Public Relations** at **443.858.2684**.

We broadcast the **"BlackUSA.News Morning Show"** Monday thru Friday from 10 to 11 am (EST) and evening programming from 7 to 8 pm (EST): **"Town Hall" with Chap & Friends** (Mondays); **"I'm Party Marty: LET'S TALK!"** (Tuesdays); **"Sistabiz" with Nicole Orr and Tamara Brown** (Wednesdays); **"Black Business Roundable"** with **Doug Blacksher** and **Everett Butler** LIVE from Oakland (Thursdays); **BlackUSA Crypto News** with DEFI expert **Kamal R. Hubbard** (Fridays). The broadcasts are LIVE and appear on YouTube.com/

doniglover, Facebook.com/bmorenewsdotcom and on Facebook/blackusanews.

Remember, we are all Black Wall Street. We all have a role to play. We are all important. Every man, woman and child in the community must be involved, if we are to succeed. And if we keep God first through it all, we can do anything but fail. Yes, we might stumble the first time. So what! Try again! And again! Get back up. Refocus. Go back to the drawing board. Try it again and again until you get it right. Make your own luck by being so good at what you do that your opposition will even hire you! And only surround yourself with people with a similar passion and positive vibrations, like my book publication team – including Pamela Reaves, Marcus Murchison, and the incomparable Frank Johnson.

Yes! All of the answers to all of the challenges we face are already inside of us. We just have to sit still sometimes ... and listen. I also believe in divine timing. And I believe in my abilities. I believe I can make a plan, stick to it, adjust and get help when necessary, and persevere through, over, under and around hell or highwater until the mission is accomplished. **I AM BLACK WALL STREET!**

When you hear of Black Wall Street, what's the first thing that pops up in your mind? Tulsa, Oklahoma, May 31 to June 1, 1921: It was one of the deadliest race riots in America, where more than 800 people were injured. The exact number of the dead may never be accurate, but the toll on the community of Tulsa, this vibrant Black community, is and was clear: Total devastation! There in the gap of Greenwood, Archer, and Pine lay a fine example of what we as a people can do, if and when left alone. And though Tulsa laid in ruin, we weren't done.

The concept of a Black Wall Street was much larger than Tulsa. And our people were too strong to let Tulsa be our ending. We didn't just have a Black Wall Street in Tulsa, OK. Black Wall Streets existed every place that Black people were due to the disenfranchisement and racists laws that governed the everyday lives of the majority of Black people in this country. It wasn't as if we could just go downtown and buy our goods like the white majority. We had to use a side entrance, if we were allowed in at all. We couldn't try on our shoes. Most often we had to trace our feet and pass the traced paper to a white salesperson who would get you what you needed. Notably, we couldn't eat at some lunch counters, nor sleep in certain hotels, but we didn't give up nor go without. We made our own.

Since the dawn of this country, people have sought to make their own way. The farmer, the blacksmith, the doctor, the painter, the mason, the butcher, the hairdresser, the tailor, and even the laborer. He or she often looked to work for someone until they were able to move on and set up shop for themselves. Think about the indentured servants or the sharecroppers of the South. They labored their way to freedom with the hopes of one day leaving a mark on this world or maybe just on this land. Others followed in their footsteps and moved the needle forward. They all reached the point in their lives where they stepped out on faith and forged their own way.

In doing so, they carry the hopes and dreams of not only themselves, but our ancestors. The spirit of making a way out of no way is something to be honored, while the lessons learned along the way are something to be shared. It is that work that makes us a community. When we fall back to the basics of each one reaching one to teach one, we build a legacy that will echo for generations to come.

We free ourselves to be bigger and better than we would ever be alone and pass that freedom on to those who are bold enough to listen, learn, and want to move the banner even higher. There's nothing more enriching than seeing a single mother or father building a legacy for their children. Or the face of a young man or woman, removed from society into the penal system, for a mistake that they made, return to become a productive citizen because someone gave them a chance that they would have otherwise not gotten.

That's what entrepreneurs do. That is the value that they add to our collective.

The purpose of the I am Black Wall Street Foundation, Inc. is to preserve our history and to help empower Black business owners and those who support them, no matter race, creed, nor national origin. We push doing business collectively/cooperative economics (ujamaa, a Kwanzaa principle). We've traveled to New Orleans, Atlanta, Richmond, New York City, Las Vegas, Washington D.C., and, of course, Baltimore, our home, where we work to spread this message of unity, economic cooperation, and love. And we will continue to cross this great nation carrying that message to all who will hear us because we are about putting in the work that brings about positive change within our community.

Lee Vaughan, Chairman, I Am Black Wall Street Foundation

Notes

The Gap Band. "You Dropped A Bomb On Me", track #6 on Gap Band IV, Total Experience Records, 1982, compact disc.

Evans, Erin. 2021. "For Black Americans, The White Terror In D.C. Looks Familiar". Huffington Post. January 7, 2021, accessed May 2, 2021. https://www.huffpost.com/entry/white-terror-capitol-riots-america_n_5ff7802ac5b6644fa210a0a7?ncid=APPLENEWS00001.

DeSantis, John. 2006. "Wilmington, N.C., Revisits a Bloody 1898 Day." The New York Times, pp. 1 and 33, June 4, 2006, accessed May 2, 2021. https://www.nytimes.com/2006/06/04/us/04wilmington.html.

Lafrance, Adrienne and Van Newkirk. 2017. The Lost History of an American Coup D'État: Republicans and Democrats in North Carolina are locked in a battle over which party inherits the shame of Jim Crow. The Atlantic. August 12, 2017, accessed May 2, 2021.

https://www.theatlantic.com/politics/archive/2017/08/wilmington-massacre/536457/.

Griffith, D. W. 1915. The Birth of a Nation. Directed by D. W. Griffith. David W. Griffith Corporation. Hollywood. February 8, 1915.

Hicks, Helena. 2014. "Dr. Helena Hicks, Erich March at 'Spirituals' Black History Program". February 24, 2014, accessed May 2, 2021. https://www.youtube.com/watch?v=oT7iHLZnkF4.

Mohamud, Naima. 2019. "Is Mansa Musa the richest man who ever lived?". BBC Africa. March 10, 2019, accessed May 2, 2021. https://www.bbc.com/news/world-africa-47379458.

Sullivan, Walter. 1985. 6th-Century Manuscript Adds to Mystery of Star. New York Times. November 18, 1985, accessed May 2, 2021. https://www.nytimes.com/1985/11/18/us/6th-century-manuscript-adds-to-mystery-of-star.html.

Welsing, Frances Cress. 2004. Isis Papers. New York: CW Publishing.

DeGruy, Joy. Post Traumatic Slave Syndrome: America's Legacy of Enduring Injury and Healing. 2017. Atlanta: Joy DeGruy Publications Inc.

History.com. 2009. Marcus Garvey. November 9, 2009, accessed May 2, 2021. https://www.history.com/topics/black-history/marcus-garvey.

Pharrell. "Entrepreneur". The Neptunes, 2020, compact disc.

Coogler, Ryan. 2018. Black Panther. Directed by Ryan Coogler. Burbank. January 29, 2018.

Saint-Vil, Sweenie. 2021. Master P reacts to Clubhouse being worth $1 billion. January 25, 2021, accessed May 2, 2021. Revolt.tv. https://www.revolt.tv/news/2021/1/25/22249100/master-p-club-house-one-billion.

BBC. 2018. "Brazil museum fire: Prized 'Luzia' fossil skull recovered." October 20, 2018, accessed May 3, 2021. https://www.bbc.com/news/world-latin-america-45926733

Connor, Steve. 2011. "World's most ancient race traced in DNA study." October 23, 2011, accessed May 3, 2021. https://www.independent.co.uk/news/science/world-s-most-ancient-race-traced-dna-study-1677113.html

Bob Marley and The Wailers. "War", track #4, side 2 on Rastaman Vibrations, Island Records, 1976, record.

Jones, Jae. 2018. "True First Americans: Califians (Khalifians) and the Poisonous Thanksgiving". November 14, 2018, accessed May 3, 2021. https://blackthen.com/true-first-americans-califians-khalifians-and-the-poisonous-thanksgiving/

Pearson, Esther. 2021. "The BlackUSA.News Morning Show, 2.19.21: Dr. Esther Pearson & Judge Leonia Lloyd". February 19, 2021, accessed May 3, 2021. https://www.youtube.com/watch?v=3DFwX-AwEL50.

Pearson, Esther. 2019. Black and Red Roots: Discovering Your Native American Ancestry. Newton: Independent.

Sertima, Ivan Van. 1991. "The Golden Age of the Moor." Journal of African Civilizations 11, Fall 1991.

Cassidy, Vincent H. deP. 1959. "Columbus and the Negro". The Phylon Quarterly Vol. 20, No. 3, 3rd Qtr., 1959.

Gerhard, Peter. 1978. "A Black Conquistador in Mexico," The Hispanic American Historical Review, Vol. 58, No. 3 (August 1978), pp. 451-459.

Herrick, Dennis (2018). Esteban: The African Slave Who Explored America. Albuquerque: University of New Mexico Press.

Osburn, Katherine M.B. 2010. "Any Sane Person": Race, Rights, and Tribal Sovereignty in the Construction of the Dawes Rolls for the Choctaw Nation. October 2010, accessed May 3, 2021. https://www.jstor.org/stable/20799406?seq=1.

Kiste, John Van der. 2018. Sarah Forbes Bonetta: Queen Victoria's African Princess. Scotts Valley: CreateSpace Independent Publishing Platform.

Brockell, Gillian, "Before 1619, there was 1526: The mystery of the first enslaved Africans in what became the United States". Washington Post. September 7, 2019.

Landers, Jane. 1990. "Gracia Real de Santa Teresa de Mose: A Free Black Town in Spanish Colonial Florida". The American Historical Review. February 1990.

Roncace, Kelly. 2016. "Black History Month: 11 things you may not know about N.J.'s history". February 8, 2016, accessed May 3, 2021. https://www.nj.com/entertainment/2016/02/important_nj_people_and_places_in_black_history.html#:~:text=Burlington%20and%20the%20Delaware%20Valley,a%20pacesetter%20in%20black%20emancipation.

Lavina, Javier. 2016. "Don Luis de Mozambique, el que elegido fue de su rebelión por rey primero Santiago del Príncipe, primer pueblo de negros libres de América". 2016, accessed May 3, 2021. https://books.google.com/books?id=bT-kIcHro18oC&pg=PA81&dq=yoruba+in+panama&hl=en#v=onepage&q=hausa&f=false.

Bayano "y los panamenos en los mediados del siglo". Hombre y Cultura. Revista del Centro de Investigaciones Antropologicas, Volume 3. El Centro: Universidad de Panama. December 1975.

Tardieu, Jean-Pierre. 2009. Cimarrones de Panamá: la forja de una identidad afroamericana en el siglo XVI. Madrid: Iberoamericana.

Haley, Alex. 1976. Roots. Directed by Marvin Chomsky. Hollywood. January 23, 1977.

Simón, Pedro (1627). Noticias historiales de Venezuela. Fundación Biblioteca Ayachucho

Pike, Ruth. 2007. "Black Rebels: The Cimarrones of Sixteenth-Century Panama". The Americas. October 2007, accessed May 5, 2021. https://www.jstor.org/stable/30139087

Gallup-Diaz, Ignacio. 2010. "A Legacy of Strife: Rebellious Slaves in Sixteenth-Century Panamá". Colonial Latin American Review 19, no. 3. 2010, accessed May 5, 2021. https://repository.brynmawr.edu/cgi/viewcontent.cgi?article=1016&context=history_pubs

Landers, Jane, "The Material Culture of the Maroons: The Cases of Ecuador, Hispaniola, Mexico and Colombia" in Rina Cáceres (comp.), Routes of Slavery in Africa and Latin America. San Jose, University of Costa Rica, 2001, pp.145-156.

Lawo Sukam, Alain, "Black Kings and African Colonial Identity in The History of Venezuela of Fray Pedro de Aguado and News Histories of the Conquests of the Mainland of Fray Pedro Simón" in Iberoamerican Magazine,vol. 72, n. 215-216, (Abr-sep, 2006), pp. 575-586.

Martínez Montiel, Luz María (coord.), African presence in South America. Mexico City, National Council for Culture and the Arts, 1995.

Miguel Guacama Rodríguez, Junius P. (2006). Encyclopedia of Slave Resistance and Rebellion, Vol. 1. Greenwood Publishing Group.

Prada, Natalia Silva. 2013. "Reyes africanos en Iberoamérica". Los Reinos de las Indias en el Nuevo Mundo. November 5, 2013, accessed May 6, 2021. https://losreinosdelasindias.hypotheses.org/523.

Kent, R. K. 2009. "Palmares: An African State in Brazil". Journal of African History. Cambridge. January 2, 2009.

Campbell, Mavis Christine. 1990. The Maroons of Jamaica, 1655-1796 : a history of resistance, collaboration & betrayal. Trenton: African World Press.

Bell, Madison Smartt. 2008. Toussaint L'Ouverture: A Biography. New York: Vintage Books.

James, C. L. R. 1989. The Black Jacobins: Toussaint L'Ouverture and the San Domingo Revolution. New York: Vintage Books.

"The History of Gullah: An Intriguing Culture of the Sea Islands". 2013. GullahHeritage.com. December 22, 2013, accessed May 7, 2021. https://www.pawleysisland.com/blog/history-of-the-gullah-culture/

Polascak, Marissa. 2019. "History of the Gullah Culture". PawleysIsland.com. https://www.pawleysisland.com/blog/history-of-the-gullah-culture/

"The Stono Rebellion 1739". PBS. https://www.pbs.org/wgbh/aia/part1/1p284.html.

"September 1739: Stono Rebellion in South Carolina". October 14, 2013 at the Wayback Machine. History in the Heartland. Ohio Historical Society, accessed May 7, 2021. https://web.archive.org/web/20131014022210/http://ww2.ohiohistory.org/historyintheheartland/timeline/timeline_display.cfm?ID=71

Thornton, John K. 1991. "African Dimensions of the Stono Rebellion". The American Historical Review Vol. 96, No. 4. Oxford University Press. October 1991.

Smith, Gene Allen. 2018. "Series: Fighting for Freedom: African Americans and the War of 1812. Sanctuary in the Spanish Empire: An African American officer earns freedom in Florida." National Park Service. https://www.nps.gov/articles/sanctuary-in-the-spanish-empire.htm.

Smith, Gene Allen. 2018. "Series: Fighting for Freedom: African Americans and the War of 1812 Sanctuary in the Spanish Empire: An African American officer earns freedom in Florida". National Park Service. August 17, 2018, accessed May 8, 2021. https://www.nps.gov/articles/sanctuary-in-the-spanish-empire.htm

Bullock, James. 2008. "Fort Mose, Florida (1738-1820)". Black Past. https://www.blackpast.org/african-american-history/fort-mose-florida/

Porter, Kenneth Williams. 2013. The Black Seminoles: History of a Freedom-Seeking People. Gainesville: University of Florida Press.

May, Jon D. 2009. "Horse, John," The Encyclopedia of Oklahoma History and Culture, https://www.okhistory.org/publications/enc/entry.php?entry=HO033.

Porter, Kenneth Williams. 1947. "Farewell to John Horse: An Episode of Seminole Negro Folk History". Phylon. Clark-Atlanta University. https://doi.org/10.2307/272343.

Porter-Mitchell, Juliette. 2012. "Story of John Horse, a Black Seminole warrior". Catholic Review. January 19, 2012. https://www.archbalt.org/story-of-john-horse-a-black-seminole-warrior/

Mulroy, Kevin. 2017. "The Seminole Freedmen: A History". Texas Ranger Review. Texas Ranger Association Foundation. http://www.texasranger.org/wp-content/uploads/2017/07/History-Seminole-Freedmen.pdf.

Johnson, Hannibal B. "The All-Black Towns in Oklahoma." The All-Black Towns in Oklahoma, 31 Dec. 2004, www.hannibalbjohnson.com/the-all-black-towns-in-oklahoma/.

Sturgis, Amy. 2012. "Black Seminoles and the Largest Slave Revolt in U.S. History". Learn Liberty. https://www.youtube.com/watch?v=5E0j8xgxjTY

Ferguson, Wes. 2019. "Why This Mexican Village Celebrates Juneteenth: Descendants of slaves who escaped across the southern border observe Texas's emancipation holiday with their own unique traditions". Texas Monthly. June 19, 2019. https://www.texasmonthly.com/being-texan/mexican-village-juneteenth-celebration/.

Mountjoy, Shane (2009). Manifest Destiny: Westward Expansion. Infobase Publishing.

Bordewich, Fergus M. 2009. "John Brown's Day of Reckoning: The abolitionist's bloody raid on a federal arsenal at Harpers Ferry 150 years ago set the stage for the Civil War". Smithsonian Magazine. https://www.smithsonianmag.com/history/john-browns-day-of-reckoning-139165084/

Wills, Shomari. 2018. Black Fortunes: The Story of the First Six African Americans Who Escaped Slavery and Became Millionaires. New York: Amistad Press.

Roberson, Jere. "McCabe, Edward P". The Encyclopedia of Oklahoma History and Culture. https://www.okhistory.org/publications/enc/entry.php?entry=MC006.

Roberson, Jere. 1973. "Edward P. McCabe and the Langston Experiment". The Chronicles of Oklahoma 51. Fall 1973.

Krehbiel, Randy. "1867 vision for what's now Oklahoma was an all-Black Territory of Lincoln". Tulsa World. November 27, 2020.

Watts, Elena. 2018. "Documenting Historic Black Settlements In Texas: A Texas A&M professor's Texas Freedom Colonies Project will help African-American Texans reclaim their unrecognized and unrecorded heritage". Texas A&M Today. October 8, 2018.

Sitton, Thad. 2005. Freedom Colonies: Independent Black Texans in the Time of Jim Crow. Austin: University of Texas Press.

Umoh, Ruth. 2020. "Black Women Were Among The Fastest-Growing Entrepreneurs—Then Covid Arrived". Forbes. October 26, 2020.

Tennyson, Alfred Lord. 1842. "Ulysses". *Poems*. London.

Logan, Harold L. "Minority Business Elixir Still Eludes Government". Washington Post. November 26, 1977.

Xion, Abraham. 2020. "The Father of the 8(a) Program: Congressman Parren J. Mitchell". February 16, 2020. https://www.linkedin.com/pulse/man-responsible-more-black-millionaires-abraham-xiong/

Clay, William L. 2000. *Just Permanent Interests*. New York: HarperCollins.

Cotter, Sean Philip. 2021. "Minority groups file discrimination complaint against Boston over contract procurement". *Boston Herald*. February 17, 2021.